Hatred of Translation

Courly rouge du Brésil, de l'âge de trois ans.

NATHANAËL

Hatred of Translation

NIGHTBOAT BOOKS

New York

Copyright © 2019 Nathanaël

ISBN: 978-1-64362-003-9

Design and typesetting by Kit Schluter
Text set in scans of Olivetti Studio 44 typewritten text,
Adobe Caslon Pro, & Futura

Cataloging-in-publication data is available from the Library of Congress

Nightboat Books
New York

www.nightboat.org

On ne peut pas devenir fou dans une époque forcenée bien qu'on puisse être brûlé vif par un feu dont on est l'égal.

RENÉ CHAR

This work is marked by a deep fault line. In many respects it is of little consequence, and naming it may only intensify the kinds of pressures that are already weighing on the fragile bodies constellated in the various midsts that are, daily, broken apart by wars (but not only) borne by avarice and fear, the pernicious quality of which suffuses the ground waters and the skies that uproot the trees and the houses against which they lean. It is impossible not to measure the consequence of one's actions and inactions and the effects of one's deliberations. Certainly, if 2016 marked some kind of limit, it was only because of the seemingly permanent dismissal of everyday atrocity—I don't mean bombs in the métro and presidents full of fatal promises— but the scratches on the lens of the quotidian, so habitual that one scarcely notices a stain in the field of one's vision, and perhaps even welcomes it as a form of indulgence. The shortcomings by which one lives may well be historical, and the fist raised in indignation may be just another desperate gesture, the collective effect of which is grotesquely insufficient—because, no doubt, of its excess, the measure of war that it promulgates. In the absence of a single place, one may not lay claim to a single origin. And in the absence of a country against which to align one's proclivities, there persist the intimate traversals of continents and the constant threat of drowning (being drowned).

November

In the course of two weeks, I slept in three cities, one of which granted me anonymity, the second, enmity, and the third an unhoped-for geology. Crumbling, calcareous rock bitten by the salted sea, and stiff with astragalus, and gulls the size of foxes who have since been assigned a sudden death count. Fig trees and grey herons and a fortressed museum. A death mask and a spitting loudspeaker to which none give heed, adjudicating misery.

In each city it rained, and the rain came in, through the ceiling or over the door, and the man sat up all night watching a bucket fill and emptying it. A small tap in the courtyard provided water until the severed pipe was repaired and the wall closed over.
Five sentinels patrolled a single cobbled square in the tourist quarter.
And the meaning assigned to liberty was once again measured against its threat, and so consigned.

Translation only ever gives the illusion of being transitive. It is always looking over its shoulder. It doesn't drift, it bolts; it doesn't flounder, it sinks. And when it runs it takes everything with it.
That this should be a means by which to account for a disappearance is not particularly revealing. But that it should make a claim for a body lost to its language is indicative at least of an important absence, that must be cultivated, for the sake of its vitality.
Perhaps it is that in accounting for translation—in attempting to do so—something fundamental is dislodged, and that is a conviction resting in an idea of *radicality*. The radical is no

stranger to grammar, which has placed its entire emphasis in it, constellating itself around such foundments, and verifying its turns against its unshakeable root (not revolutionary, or else yes: predictably—no, murderously, so).

Hatred of Translation writes itself against the idea of such a root, and finds itself to be complicit with Emanuele Coccia's caution against exactly this tendency: "We continue to conceive of ourselves through the prism of a falsely *radical* model, we continue to think the living and its culture through a false image of roots (because isolated from the rest). As though, by thinking the root as reason, we had transformed reason itself and thought into a blind force of rootedness, into the faculty of the construction of a cosmic tie with the earth. In this sense, the replacement of the model of the classic root system with that of the rhizome does not represent a veritable change of paradigm: thought continues to be what allows us to think the Earth, and only the Earth, as *ground* [...]."[1] When Coccia places the sun back in the sky,[2] when he returns the earth to its astral dimension, stripping occidental thought of its geo-centrism, he hands his readers the earth's contingency: "Not inhabitable by definition," he affirms.

As Gilles Clément contends, "we breathe water."[3] So the sky is the earth's pool, and the stars are its liquid eyes.
In the month of May of this writing, the trees have not yet leaved; the swallows have flown past the city, and the migrations have been driven beyond their reach.

---

1.   Emanuele Coccia. *La vie des plantes*. Éditions Payot & Rivages. Paris, 2016 (116-117).

2.   As did Simone Weil before him, to the tree: *L'arbre est en vérité enraciné dans le ciel. (The tree is in truth rooted in the sky). La personne et le sacré.* Éditions Payot & Rivages. Paris, 2017 (60).

3.   Gilles Clément. *Nuages*. Bayard. Paris, 2005 (11).

If I have lived with and sometimes inside translation, I may say with certainty that I have never inhabited it, anymore than it me. And that the threatened ecologies of human stupidity are intricated in the permanent work of repatriation which governs so much of what calls itself translation.

There is insurance for such things now as repatriation, and some governments, which imagine themselves to represent the peoples of free countries, require such documentation of its visitors: but it is not ever made clear whether repatriation anticipates a route of return to the living or the dead. From this vantage, the borders are all closed, and each voyage signifies a defeat for the traveller and a condemnation of those who have already gone missing.

Long before me, Ingeborg Bachmann spoke out for the camel. Élisée Reclus deplored the razing of the marshes of the new world and its assassinated creature.
It was a philosopher who cut open the stomach of a turtle to watch its heart beat.

Let this be my testimony to the separation of the ages.

Nathanaël
Chicago
May, 2019

TABLE

Dispatch for an Early Grave

I don't know if this is a letter I am capable of writing. If one is the sum of one's suffering, the realization that comes of recognizing one's sufferings to be generalizable acts as a sort of annulment. And the fields grossly ploughed by the slaughtered beasts in waiting prove just as stricken with terror and just as saturated with blood as those one comes only to read about. It is past the point of decrying the error of human waste, and past the point of revelling in a kind of exacerbated subjectivity, where the self-same is the condition of a voided contract with history. No one ever sees it coming but this is only a measure of a capacity for disbelief and a willingness to be lied to. And one is always ever and none. The author of a disappointment. Caught between a decision and a choice. It wasn't ever for me to say. And the crass forms of lineage that scaffold the way into and out of one's pain are the outline also of a murder committed in permanence. One needn't the death camp as a model nor S-21 nor Guantánamo Bay. The name alone suffices. For as many borders as are crossed there are bodies left hanging. The human taste has consistently been for exemplarity. And the examples abound, in the variegated narratives of mute extermination, and the supremacies that vociferously command them. In the too-closed mouth one finds an appetite for distinction, and an enumeration of bodies. Over the fields of solar panels lie miles and miles of murdered skies. And the hands at the ends of arms that belong to bodies can scarcely hold the remainder of a single integer. So it rips up the roots and proclaims the living dead. Language is a stinking compost heap set ablaze by fuming methane, setting off smoke that stings the eyes and turns the livid faces blind. Insomnia is an inverted narcolepsy, the mind trained on a vapid darkness populated with tirades and dread, and the threshold come morning burns under a sun liberated from a thousand tyrannies only to ignite a thousand more. And so the body runs. Up and over and under the gun. And so it cries out *Kill me!* To stand apart is also an act of solidarity. A refusal of libidinous gods and childhoods given to feeding them. Despotism has always served as security for the weak-minded who want the corral with the bull and its evisceration. To pull the bones from the living skeleton. To strip the skin of its layers of flesh. And make dust of the rest. What kind of letter could ever come of this if not one of tantalized condemnation? The tungsten filaments have been secreted away. And filial indiscretion is at its acme. Who hasn't been shamed by the everyday? Dumbstruck by the vicissitudes that produce the most incestuous of falsehoods, with the bed sheet as its witness. If one cried out in agony, the jury would be satisfied, the estate sold, and the matter put to rest. You jest! What agonies subsist in the dull, impatient corridors? Who hear the dead scream anymore? This is a tempered age of obedience. Of fists driven into one's own throat. And self-prescribed barbiturates at evening. The calamity was long scripted, as well as its survival. For every body washed up on the shore there is a narrative of oblivion. These must be the nominal freedoms. The manuscripts of Portbou and the grassy graves of Oujda, where the names are written out. What were the singing stones to the scattered limbs of Orpheus? "I was such an orphan as never learned to love."

(January 21, 2017)

6

Augustment
(Translation without Language)

La liberté n'est pas ce qu'on nous montre sous ce nom. Quand l'imagination, ni sotte, ni vile n'a, la nuit tombée, qu'une parodie de fête devant elle, la liberté n'est pas de lui jeter n'importe quoi pour tout infecter. La liberté protège le silence, la parole et l'amour. Assombris, elle les ravive; elle ne les macule pas. Et la révolte la ressuscite à l'aurore, si longue soit celle-ci à s'accuser. La liberté, c'est de dire la vérité, avec des précautions terribles, sur la route où TOUT se trouve.

RENÉ CHAR, 1958

"Se le puede echar la culpa de todo."

JUAN ANTONIO BARDEM
Muerte de un ciclista, 1955

„ It is a point of fact that one is more likely to walk away from the body in the road, than toward it. I can provide several instances of this, none of which can be corroborated, today: a pigeon on a late afternoon in winter, twitching on a sidewalk, its chest feathers gored, and the people with their mocking grimaces; an overturned car in the Indre region of France in the late eighties, a small car, blood, there is blood on the windows, and one needn't imagine the bodies, besides, they are not visible from the road; a bus stop in Lyon, young fascists, and a homeless man, the fists seem to be striking nothing, over and over. When the fist strikes me, I am able to attest to this beating silence.

„ Why begin with the pigeon.

„ It is possible, with Spinoza, to regard it as a "universal failing in people that they communicate their thoughts to others." One must, in such an instance, understand *communication* as an *a priori* failing of truth. Exacerbated, as it is by desire, and the desire to contain it. The silence that is called for authenticates what *might be said*. It recognizes as something more than the mere futility of speaking, but rather the danger of giving one's voice so off-handedly to language.

„ There is no obvious equivalency between truth and language. Nor is there evidence that one may be divined from the other. If truth is what is not able to be brought to language, then language must be understood as, if not a form of, then an instrument of, justice. Or, justice itself.**

„ Language is a capital crime. It is always truth that is hanged at dawn. Followed by several austere pronouncements.

„ 'A body beneath a head.'

„ *Whose hand rattles the door at midnight?* In crimes of passion, there are no mistakes. What is mistaken is the motive, again and again. The hand rattles the door because something has been shut out. Because the body is skin is pores is postulate. The desire to sing is the same as the desire to bleed or to disintegrate. With the freedom to speak comes the freedom not to speak. Too much has been said already. In the compulsive confessional.

„ There is a variety of hibiscus that carries the name of Joan of Arc. Not far from where the mourning doves gather under a mulberry tree. A tree that is exchangeable for a continent. A chimney for eaves. A name for nothing.

„ Truth accuses itself. It is the body in the road. And as far as one is willing to walk. That tribunal.

„ If I wish to speak of freedom why speak of truth. This is my nod to obsolescence. Desuetude.

„ Violence is as much in the injunction to speak as it is in its prohibition. I am interested in neither of these. What *ought* and *ought not*.

„ The throat had sedimented thought.

„ There is no such word as *augustment* in English.* Still there is an alternance in the leaf's permeation. A flood to stop the rains at autumn. A hardening of the membrane. And the plant's mitigated injury at winter. In this instance, when it is struck, the sound is caught inside the cell without reverberation.

„ *Dear friend, augusted is not demise, but premonition. A feather floating over a sewer.*

„ In the impermanent graft of languages, the lie becomes apparent (—*ment*, you could say, is not what I *meant*, but that didn't prevent it from being said). The promise of a 'day without consequence' is the admission of the day's fallibility, and its failure at averting disaster. August is a month of many months, replete with undiagnosable futures. It has this to say about history:

„ The misadequated elegy despises living.

„ The continent is adrift, and with your two legs on either antiquated shore, you choose severance, and thirst. The mind drafted into this thinking dreams screaming of these same bureaucracies. It wants to know what it is capable of.

„ In the misadventures of the speaker, there is no telling what happens. The time that would account for it is suspended in water, between air and ice, with its mistakenness and candour.

„ We are a far-flung body. A massive misalignment. In the truculence of verbiage, the absence of sentience. And the quick to sentencing.

„ Each time a door opens, it fails at being a wall.

Augustment (bis)

„ It is a point of fact that one is more likely to walk away from the body in the road, than toward it. I can provide several instances of this, none of which can be corroborated, today: a pigeon on a late afternoon in winter, twitching on a sidewalk, its chest feathers gored, and the people with their mocking grimaces; an overturned car in the Indre region of France in the late eighties, a small car, blood, there is blood on the windows, and one needn't imagine the bodies, besides, they are not visible from the road; a bus stop in Lyon, young fascists, and a homeless man, the fists seem to be striking nothing, over and over. When the fist strikes me, I am able to attest to this beating silence.

„ Why begin with the pigeon.

„ It is possible, with Spinoza, to regard it as a "universal failing in people that they communicate their thoughts to others." One must, in such an instance, understand *communication* as an *a priori* failing of truth. Exacerbated, as it is by desire, and the desire to contain it. The silence that is called for authenticates what *might be said*. It recognizes as something more than the mere futility of speaking, but rather the danger of giving one's voice so off-handedly to language.

„ There is no obvious equivalency between truth and language. Nor is there evidence that one may be divined from the other.

If truth is what is not able to be brought to language, then language must be understood as, if not a form of, then an instrument of, justice. Or, justice itself.**

„ Language is a capital crime. It is always truth that is hanged at dawn. Followed by several austere pronouncements.

„ 'A body beneath a head.'

„ *Whose hand rattles the door at midnight?* In crimes of passion, there are no mistakes. What is mistaken is the motive, again and again. The hand rattles the door because something has been shut out. Because the body is skin is pores is postulate. The desire to sing is the same as the desire to bleed or to disintegrate. With the freedom to speak comes the freedom not to speak. Too much has been said already. In the compulsive confessional.

„ There is a variety of hibiscus that carries the name of Joan of Arc. Not far from where the mourning doves gather under a mulberry tree. A tree that is exchangeable for a continent. A chimney for eaves. A name for nothing.

„ Truth accuses itself. It is the body in the road. And as far as one is willing to walk. That tribunal.

„ If I wish to speak of freedom why speak of truth. This is my nod to obsolescence. Desuetude.

„ Violence is as much in the injunction to speak as it is in its prohibition. I am interested in neither of these. What *ought* and *ought not*.

„ The throat had sedimented thought.

„ There is no such word as *augustment* in English.* Still there is an alternance in the leaf's permeation. A flood to stop the rains at autumn. A hardening of the membrane. And the plant's mitigated injury at winter. In this instance, when it is struck, the sound is caught inside the cell without reverberation.

„ *Dear friend, augusted is not demise, but premonition. A feather floating over a sewer.*

„ In the impermanent graft of languages, the lie becomes apparent (—*ment*, you could say, is not what I *meant*, but that didn't prevent it from being said). The promise of a 'day without consequence' is the admission of the day's fallibility, and its failure at averting disaster. August is a month of many months, replete with undiagnosable futures. It has this to say about history:

„ The misadequated elegy despises living.

„ The continent is adrift, and with your two legs on either antiquated shore, you choose severance, and thirst. The mind drafted into this thinking dreams screaming of these same bureaucracies. It wants to know what it is capable of.

„ In the misadventures of the speaker, there is no telling what happens. The time that would account for it is suspended in water, between air and ice, with its mistakenness and candour.

„ We are a far-flung body. A massive misalignment. In the truculence of verbiage, the absence of sentience. And the quick to sentencing.

„ Each time a door opens, it fails at being a wall.

(August 8, 2014)

to DE

impetus

Char: Liberty is not what one is shown by this name. When imagination, neither foolish, nor vile, has, at nightfall, only a parody of a feast before it, liberty is not to throw anything at it to infect it all. Liberty protects silence, speech and love. Darkened, they are enlivened by it; it does not stain them. And revolt resuscitates it at dawn, however long it takes for it to accuse itself. Liberty, is to say the truth, with terrible precautions, on the road on which ALL is found.

Bardem: "You can blame everything on it."

proviso

* *"Aoûtement. Une dimension franchit le fruit de l'autre."* René Char, 1938.
** *"Il y a des crimes de passion et des crimes de logique."* Albert Camus, 1951.

contention

"And Camus's 'justice' was a concept forged and betrayed in Europe," James Baldwin, 1972.

In the designation of the topography of a bird, a significant error is only alluded to: that of the bird's flight. Take for example, the kestrel's wing, with its accented feather, as a vestige of a body on a beach. Martial suggestion is of no use here; the primordial matter is silence. If the film is run once through the projector, the sound of the projector, now removed, signifies only the film. Run through a second time, it is a fanciful reprise. In drawing the contour of a city or a square, nothing is left to the imagination. The wing is an actual wing, torn from the body of a small bird of prey on an overpopulated bluff, and seen by no one. If the wing is said to be a version, then everything is permitted.

(October)

Hatred of Translation

Il me semblait qu'à la poésie véritable accédait seule la haine.

GEORGES BATAILLE

La traduction des petits textes d'Hans-Georg: la torture, l'impression finale que ce texte m'appartient tout en étant mon ennemi.

HERVÉ GUIBERT

Discretion and Fury

] In 1947, Georges Bataille published a confidential book entitled *La haine de la poésie*. For its republication by Éditions de Minuit in 1962, he retitled it *L'impossible*, evoking the opacity of its former title, which had remained incomprehensible to his readership. *À peu près personne ne comprit le sens du premier titre, c'est pourquoi je préfère à la fin parler de* L'impossible.[1] No less *impossible* than the first title, the author's concession seems to choke on its desire for accession, in other words, disappointment.

But *L'impossible* might function as a rejoinder to a form of impassibility, as though a gesture of discretion (and fury, no doubt) at the exposed ossature, just as its remains continue to be invisible. An inside, as it were, turned out. Bataille's public was no more illumined as a result of this accommodation. And a tear had been made visible in the author's vestment.

>] *The history of translation is full of such correctives. Recall that Jacques Derrida's adoption of the now much-abused term* déconstruction, *at the time a re-introduction of the vocable into the French lexicon, arose out of the difficulty of translating*

---

1. *Almost no one understood the meaning of the first title, which is why I prefer finally to speak of* The Impossible. Tr. Robert Hurley.

the German Destruktion. *There is almost no trace left now of Derrida's first decision, which was to translate* Destruktion—*a term more proximately aligned with an architecturally inflected idea of destructuring—by the misdecided and subsequently elided* destruction.

Embedded in the translative act is not only a subdued destructive force, but an act of concealment, of its own archive, of resistance, why not, to itself. [2

Contra Translation
(for the admission of light and air)

] I wish to speak ill of translation and of translators.

] Call it a *professional deformation*, to abuse, for a moment, the French phrase. In the light of the contemporary pious consensus destined to the martyred translator for undertaking the often anonymous traversal of borders between languages, weighted with pacific significance as the rent frontiers of nations are more explicitly bloodied than they have allowed themselves to be in at least as many years as it has been since the recognized tellers of history have acknowledged the existence of concurrent wars on territories extrinsic to their own. Just recently, Europe congratulated itself for the *absence of war* in its (divisive) lands since 39-45.

---

2. Out of a concern for (impossible) transparency, I recognize here as well, the inexplicit replacement, in a reprint of our translation (with Rachel Gontijo Araújo) of *The Obscene Madame D.* of *porcine child* with *pig child*—a partial concession to relevant criticism, though we rejected the excessive swagger of *pig-boy* to maintain at least some resonance with the Christian *child* of Hilst's implacable derision.

] But one should not overlook blaming translators themselves for the rehabilitation of their image from traitorous, loose-moralled floozies of language, to accredited diplomatic ambassadors, authorized foreign agents devoted to the open smuggling of precious cultural goods across otherwise inhospitable limits. For they are also, in conspiratorial bind with their publishers, responsible, at times collaterally, for the selective transmission of culture, producing such bibliographic lacunae as that which may lead, for example, an anglophone audience to conflate enshrined texts taught in French grammar schools (such as, for francophiles, those written by Mallarmé, Proust or Flaubert, to name but these) with the most provocative exemplars of contemporary experimentation.

] It might be more just to speak of benighted translators. The dark-souled, muddy-minded, compromission of often inscrutable, and not always pleasurable, promiscuities, which places one at odds with and in defense of the works of literature one is given to traducing.

Truth in Translation

] Translators are none other than the High Ransomers of *foreign*[3] cultures. In the process of holding one culture ransom, they[4] find themselves brandishing ransom notes for at least as many of the cultures as are attributed to the

---

3. I insist on this particular archaism, the reinforcement of dividing lines that inevitably confound themselves in the mixage of bodies, their *transpirations*, dripping rotten succulence from their abject pores, perfidiously secretive of infection and hideous in their woundedness, manged, sucked and un-suckable.

4. I say *they* though I could just as easily say *we*—each is its own form of travesty, being neither of each and owable to nothing.

languages in which they work, exposing in the process, the *foreignness* of every culture, and their distance from what they might be inclined to call their *own*. *La torture*, writes Hervé Guibert as he undertakes to translate several texts by his friend and photographer Hans-Georg Berger, *l'impression que ce texte m'appartient tout en étant mon ennemi*.[5] And one is quickly under the spell of this admission, replete with it, and complicit with its sentiment.

] It is a signal, among other things, to his undertaker that the rot has already set in. And what rot indeed, with its transmittable indigestions, and sensorial splendours, verging on repulsion, in the exchange value of secreting bodies, such as they are designated and repeatedly repealed.

] But Guibert's pronouncement is retractable. In the subsequent paragraph[6] he turns against himself and his willingness to be marshalled into the seductive notion of the translating body as occupying a battle line, conceding a conflation of this toil with an attitude he holds against his own work: *Non, l'idée précédente du texte ennemi était séduisante, mais fausse. J'avais par rapport à ce travail*

---

5. *...a torture, the final sense that this text belongs to me just as it is my enemy.*
6. *Le mausolée des amants*, it seems necessary to again specify, is written in undated paragraphs, arranged, so the reader believes, chronologically, with an over-arching concern for the novel as a form for the journal, which was not retrieved following the author's death from a musty cupboard at the back of an abandoned house, but devised as a work in itself, a posthumous intention, the majority of which the author typed into manuscript form himself from extant notebooks. Despite a desire to romanticize these lines as the hidden text of an exposed author, one must resign oneself, alas, (I say alas for those attached to such permanent ideals of fragile beauty) to the recognition that this author had nothing to hide, and therein lies the whole of his secret.

l'attitude que j'ai avec mon propre travail, c'est-à-dire qu'au moment où je le faisais j'avais l'impression de rater ce que j'aurais pu faire, le résultat positif n'apparaît qu'une fois le travail terminé.[7] Correcting[8] his pugnacious impulse with a rationalization about a failure analogous to the labour of writing, Guibert effectively rescues himself from the dangerous fault line about which his body teeters.[9] It is a rare moment in the *Journal* in which Guibert substantiates himself out of alleged disinterest: *Mais ce genre de notation, cette recherche de précision ici ne m'intéresse pas.*[10]

] In two paragraphs dedicated to the act of translation (the only instance of this in the more than five hundred pages of the *Journal*), Guibert calls up *possession, uselessness,* and *disinterest.* This lexical combinatory is revelatory of latencies at work in the much idealized task of

---

7. *No, the previous idea of the enemy text was seductive, but false. I had in relation to that work the attitude that I have with my own work, which is to say that at the moment at which I was doing it I felt as though I was failing at what I could have done, the positive result only appears once the work is complete.*

8. Correction, pronounced in French, also means punishment, which does not exclude corporal punishment. To be corrected is (also) to be beaten (recognizing here, that the *correcteur* is also a grammarian...). Thomas Bernhard's Roithamer is surely the most relevant and explicitly convincing example of this tendency in western literature (*Korrektur*, 1975). The more capriciously detailed the plans, the more intractable the suicide. The house built for the dead, the cone-shaped non-sequitur in the midst of an otherwise protected wood, is none other than a cenotaph—a tomb (if not a hecatomb) that is empty of a body. In this instance, the cenotaph anticipates the architect's *rigor mortis*, for who else will live in the mortifically abandoned skin of a now unspoken language if not the unsubstantiably disappeared himself.

9. Of course, the labour of translation may never be pronounced terminated; contrary to a written work, it is in permanent abeyance.

10. *But this sort of notation, this search for precision here is of no interest to me.*

Übersetzung such as it presents itself, and is almost Wilde in its sentiment.[11]

] It seems self-evident that if the translator is to be blamed, so is language. In among some of the most confounding words to transpose from French into English is the seemingly innocuous preposition, *de*. (Prepositional relations offer in fact among some of the most grievous difficulties of translation, in light, in particular, not only of the ambiguities they reveal, but of their exposure of radical differences in semantic armatures. If I were building a boat out of this work, it most surely would sink, or else become a weathervane—in any case, I would welcome the diversion…, but never would I be able to claim that *it resembled itself*). Already, in the brief catalogue of aversions assembled here, the *de*, most readily translatable as *of* has manifested itself severally, whether in the title of Guibert's journals, *Le mausolée des amants*, in Bataille's misunderstood indictment of poetry, *La haine de la poésie*, or in the title of this piece, *Hatred of Translation*. This isn't a quibble, nor is it an appeal, but the identification of a *fault* in language that takes the form of a loophole. *De* is a kind of gallows— whose particularities go too readily unidentified. *La photo de Hervé Guibert* could just as much indicate a photograph *belonging to* Guibert, a photograph *taken by* Guibert, as a photograph *in which* the author figures—disorienting the location of the now explicitly ambiguous (*self-*) portrait.[12]

---

11. Guibert's dismissiveness is inverse from Ortega y Gasset's appeal, in "Miseria y esplendor de la traducción," (1937) to an incompletable Utopian ideal, one that reaches through the knowledge of its foregone outcomes: *Parte siempre hacia el fracaso, y antes de entrar en la pelea lleva ya herida la sien.* (*He is always marching toward failure, and even before entering the fray, he already carries a wound in his temple.* Tr. E.G. Miller.)

12. Guibert, himself, troubles this distinction in the catalogue/novel, *Le*

]   *De / of* marks a demarcation line that is both intransmissible and unapproachable. This is not simple fabrication. An etymological obsolescence embedded in the English preposition *of* reveals that "the primary sense [of *of*] was 'away', 'away from' [...]."[13] Out of *of, away*. It is one manner of casting the die. Out of the body that nears its disappearance, as though out of sheer plenitude and starvation for none other than its name. If the body could be figured otherwise, it would be at a permanent horizon beyond the horizon. Not a death, but its pronouncement. In permanent compromise with itself, and in the full allowance of its execution.

]   No translator can claim the kind of exclusive proximities upheld on the name of this profession. The preposition alone rejects such a lure, and makes its measure in the way Guibert measured the photograph of the lover-friend: at arm's length, touching, and pushing *away*.[14]

]   The destructive impulse of language is irresistible. It is a way of hiding the corpse afore the fact. The stinking corpse of the murdered text run backwards through a vitriolic digestive tract, a ritual imaginable as both sodomic and vomitive, in either case, procuring pleasures undivulged, and unhoped for satiation, and always at the mercy of an intruder, oneself.

---

seul visage (*Un livre avec des figures et des lieux, n'est-ce pas un roman?*—*A book with figures and locations, is that not a novel?*)—see pp. 20 (*Moi*) and 37 (*Autoportrait*) for a rejection of the too-facile subjective associations of the *auto-retrato*. Is not the translator also translated?

13. *Oxford English Dictionary*, 2015.

14. *L'ami*, 1979.

Truth in Translation (bis)

One imagines oleanders bursting from wax leaves, a winding river recast as a Roman road and plane trees quietly furled against millenary walls, lavender by the road and flamingos, extravagantly cross with the atmosphere, while storks rap their wooden beaks and dusk settles over herons in the delicate crosshatch of trees. Instead the Roman road proves a putrescent tyranny, circumscribing histories of renewable fascisms and the body catches between a clanking courtyard that claims Van Gogh as its misery and bullrings before the likes of which Hemingway applauded. Balls, I say. Wednesdays, don't walk in the country for the hunters; and the rest of the time stay off the street. At least it isn't summer, the bull's meat, imbued with tranquillizers and Epsom salts to lull it into the bullfighter's sabre, will gorge a stomach avid for such victories as only men can wield through this kind of chemical extortion. The studio is double-decked and the wind blows in through the small porthole over the bed in the loft, resurrecting one's ghost to come. At the table on the floor, the books are arranged so as to suggest industriousness, and a tea kettle so as not to have to enter the communal kitchen, with its stink of sardines and the burnt motors of laundry machines, someone's shriek over scorched oil and someone else's progeny. This is Arles, I don't mind saying so, where the last of Guibert's body is autopsied in the final vomiting ache of a stomach cramped and belching over a toilet bowl, the mouth, a mouth in the customary way, sucking at itself, gasping its evacuations swallowed back into the chicken-necked torso of some unrecognizable rake. The trains are full of fakers and between here and the next place, there is a fight between two people and fists striking flesh until someone intervenes striking harder. I cannot find a single notation for the early part of the year, save a lone entry at December: "idiot." The rest is in the body's flight from itself, the unwritten jerk, the way a hand does as it trains itself to do, in the mesmerism of concatenated sleeps rounded to an even insomnia, the way a friend pronounces it, insonnia, somewhere between an execution and a clanging bell, striking the quarter hour, with the mouth hard around it. Well my mouth was hard around it and it didn't prevent me from lurching, the whole text in and out both ends at the same time. It was never a promise to like it, but to lie with it, in the way turtles stop in the middle of the road waiting, perhaps purposefully, to be run over, or for someone to come and lift them, gently, in arms that won't smash their shells and rip out their meat, but place them, gently, entrails and all, in the scrub on the other side, so that they can keep racking themselves over the gravel to the next place, a sea edge before the sun rises over it and the pelagic birds come hunting in droves. A translator was always a hunter, as was the photographer until the silver gelatine print was invented— at the mercy of the streams and riverbeds—and hunting, was hunted, like the most prized furs on the backs of living things. You could lie down in a translator the way you lie on a bearskin or a hot stone in summer. It's a short distance to losing one's breath, and touching, it touches what wants only to die, the way the living die, gasping, and choking themselves back. In the end, the abattoir is full of living things, don't be fooled by the signs of death, every living thing breathing in its blood, the way it comes out of the ears and feeds the existing waterways.

(March 2015)

EPIGRAPHS:

Bataille: *It seemed to me that true poetry was only reached by hatred.* (Tr. Robert Hurley.)

Guibert: *The translation of Hans-Georg's short texts: a torture, the final [impression] that this text belongs to me just as it is my enemy.*

Derelict of Duty

Os sentimentos vastos não têm nome.

Hilda Hilst

Je plonge, j'arrache avec mes ongles, là, à l'intérieur.

Danielle Collobert

If obscenity were to claim any parentage to obsolescence, it might be through an inexact filiation *i/*licited through an apprehension of language that might be qualified as *untoward*. Certainly, to insinuate myself, as I have done, and did do, into a work of lusophone disobedience, *without language*, as it were, wearing myself into its verb, is precisely the sort of act that might encourage the distribution of various punishments—*pains*, I might say—capital pains, to borrow directly from French, the language by which I came, not without complicity, to translate Hilda Hilst from Portuguese, at the close of an unread summer in a city of rains, at the edge of no place at all. The inverted cellar, opened to unnamed skies, where Madame D's agonia ransacked the inert innards of a person with no eu to speak of. It is out of that particular moment, a summer of dereliction, abandonment, and dishonesty, that D.'s letter started its slow way to English, and not without violent abandon!

A narrative, even erring and errant, into the dissuasive efforts of translation, can only obfuscate the enervated itineraries that led somehow[1] to my becoming the vessel thrown onto

---

1. It is no accident unless friendship is an accident (of course it is), and in this instance, owes everything to the prescience of Rachel Gontijo Araújo, who, through the untimely channels of a most unreliable international post,

that particularly encrypted shore. It is not mappable, any more than the route leading down the stairs between the voice of Ehud's frustrated entreaties and Madame D.'s cupboard, her chosen dwelling place, a world. Like the parchment that disintegrates in water, dispersing its direction, it finds a way nonetheless to hammer violently at a door.

E agora?

, come let's go to sleep, yes, let's go to sleep, what is Time like, Ehud, in the hole where you are now dead ?
MADAME D.

Fancying the translational dilemma that accompanies the Freudian *agora* against which none who emerges from the twentieth century has been successfully inoculated, with its suggestions of interiority as internment, and aghast proximities, positing *a disquieting strangeness*[2] against an asynchronous *disturbance*,[3] it is possible (necessary) to walk the confines of this particular duress, in order to arrive at an appropriately strait-jacketed resiliency such as exists in the scripting of the letter *D*.

---

placed, as it were, the book in the hand that would come to reach for those particularly damaged skies. By which I mean: birdlike, forlorn.

2. *L'inquiétante étrangeté*—only one of the proposed translations into French for *das Unheimlichkeit* that accosts the agora in bedridden garb, masked and insatiate, a dull cavern or exasperated expanse.

3. Italian's rejoinder to *das Unheimlichkeit* is *il perturbante*, language which bears an intensity neither the *unhomely* nor *uncanny* will ever approximate, multiplying the channels of disorientation, and exceeding the scope of its verve, further destabilising the edifice of versions, allowing for the incursion of dissimilarities in volume and mass to become visible (imaginable as bodies, in various stages of undress—or decomposition).

Agora, the wind-swept marketplace, a kind of urban desertion, is none other than the public square, theatre of a gallows circumscribed by each of four directions (but why stop at four, the circle is incommensurable with finitude)— call it *la place publique*, *forum* or assembly, what proposes itself as the (treacherous) scene of democracy unseats the diasporic discomfiture of sensation, sensate being. *Agora* is not mere *locus* but indisputable *tempus*. A gathering of anguishes subsumed into political *gravitas*, with its morbid delinquencies.

In the dictionary of meanings, the Portugese *agora* is (almost) as innocuous, as the German *heute*, brought out of its familiarity by *Malina*,[4] where the presentness of today is proposed as an exclusive signifier of suicide: self-murder. Why return to this declaration, if not to point obliquely at the significance of an agoric double-exposure, evident in the superimposition of the Greek term,[5] later inflected by Freud's diagnosis of alienation, over the Portuguese *agora*: **now**.

The composite is revelatory of cultural sedimentation, historical bed-wetting, and lyrical disembodiment. Any trace of a trace is owable to the fervent over-inscription of human felony—the fellowship of morbidity.

What is *now* in the time of translation, in the field notes of a voice afflicted with the ability to hear itself resonate, past promiscuous windowsills and into the underpants of simple-minded, prickly-groined conventicles.

---

4. Ingeborg Bachmann.

5. In *term* one cannot but concede the *terminus*, beyond which every imagined thing gropes past itself into un-conceding juris-diction.

I offer the following as testimony:

[...]

This summer will have taken the form of a decision.

[...]

It really is the end of a world, and I feel as though I am posted in Siberia or Singapore, in a strange sing-songy compound where the children carry guns in the form of balloons but the next boat out of here isn't for another month.

[...]

It's impossible, and I carry a sort of terror or detachment, a retinal disturbance that superimposes forms and moments.

[...]

Does it ever occur to psychoanalysis to say no? It seems to me just as important to recognise the hidden text as it is to resolve not to read it.

[...]

To cross the border toward your country is to leave the body of my sister, to take possession of something that escapes me. But what violence, to tear her body from mine, where it is lodged, with the other bodies gathered there.

[...]

Your face, for example.

[...]

Must I be the one to survive, not only the book, but never?

[...][6]

Translation is a form of castigation. Of language foremost, and of itself of course. In the *now time* of translation, beyond its morbid measurements, recombined into entreating narratives of diplomatic traversal, it points to the orgiastic cowardice of extinction, with wistful inexactitude.

If translation is belated (Benjamin), it is also apprehensive (Ortega y Gasset): it anticipates itself. It is its fore-knowledge which is so calamitous.

It is obsequious and fragile, and so brutal.

Now is time unbemoaned. Translation is its foment. *Por agora.*

A Capital Snare

It is no good admitting to one's inconsistencies. It makes for meagre parable and disingenuous apology. Nonetheless, if Madame D. arrived at English in a strait-jacket unamenable to divagation, it is precisely what gagged and blindfolded her text that made it legible.

If only more of us wore our skins out.

---

6. *The Middle Notebookes.* Nightboat Books. New York, 2015 (357-363). These annotations are from 2010.

É você (R.G.A.)

Wearing glasses was not for the purpose
of seeing things more clearly.
SAGAWA CHIKA, tr. Sawako Nakayasu

Coming to *A Obscena Senhora D* by way of *L'obscène Madame
D.* it is immediately clear that the effort demanded of us
is a *dispersive* more than a *discursive* one. Perhaps it is that
the *emotional* demand implicates a language in the flesh—
kneaded, knotted and bruised—that belies *comprehension.*
What I mean is that a translator's pretence to *fluency* is
corrected when faced with the evidence of exclusion. The
multiplication of versions decorticates the so-called original
to the point of burning out the incumbent text—like the
radioactive blast that photographs the city while annihilating
it.[7] The subsisting layers of civilisation, exposed under attack,
reveal themselves to be vacant craters, as wide as worlds, and
uninvested (screaming). If we walk there, we agree to our
own admonishment, and the horror induced by stray hairs.
Oxygen is two parts matter. And dirty rainfall. In the third
instance, a distortion occurs, which simultaneously renders
visible *all three languages at once*, by virtue of none of them
arriving at themselves.
With intermittence, and delay, we look at looking.[8]

—past oceans,
and shadow-pictures.*

---

7. Say "city" so as not to have to think *beings.*

8. I say *looking* and not *reading* in the way one must step back at times
in order to see better what is near. If one begins with the pretext that the
glass is *never clear,* then one begins to escape (maybe) the trappings of
occidental ideology of *intelligibility*, which lead invariably to a tendency
toward *correction.* Where grammar fails the text is precisely where such a
tendency must be identified, then rejected. From there, the best one can do
is to cast one's lot.

*

*The instrument that measures the intensity and duration
of sunshine was once referred to as a radiograph. The relay
between object and image relies on an exchange of rays between
bodies (that are at once reflective and absorptive), confounding,
in the process, the distinction between desire and Antigone,
such that the 'shadow-picture of a hand' for example, not only
accounts for the hand, but destroys it once and for all, so that
its identification relies absolutely upon its annulment.
There is a sky for everything. An upturned bank of refractive
solar panels in the Mojave Desert incinerates birds in flight.*
"A sun black with stupor."[9]

"What the Birds Knew"

Agora is a permanent remove. A storm advancing against
a force of inveterate stillness. A severed head planted on
the sharpened post of a new kind of madness. (New for
having seen it before). *Who is it in the press that calls on me?*[10]
Translation is the ravaged soothsayer, saying backwards what is.
In the rainswept *agora*, *now* is ever, for the time of its rending,
whatever the face settled into its war.

The muscle that follows is a muscle of grief.
RACHEL GONTIJO ARAÚJO

To have released Kurosawa Akira's film in English under the
title *I Live in Fear* was already an act of treason. *Ikimono no
kiroku* (1955) casts Mifune Toshiro as *the body of dread*. An
otherwise (societally) manacled dread that underwrites the
delirium of reason in the atomic tail wind. After Hiroshima

---

9. *Madame D.*
10. William S.

and Nagasaki come the Soviet land blasts, and Bikini Atoll, roiling radioactive cumulus over northern Japan, eradicating the certitude of concrete bunkers sunken in sand. Nakajima Kiichi imagines *Brasil* as promised land, an isolatable *else* without fallout, onto which he casts the intractable die—fire and stone's throw. *Love of the unknown.*

The failure of his projection owes as much to Nakajima's acuity as it does to his bad temper, in a word: *disbelief.* The imagined become unimaginable, in a juridical heavy hand that secludes him behind the carceral bars of an asylum, the man can only strike ghosts in the form of people subsumed into docility. The sun that burns the planet is as much fabrication as it is an incontrovertible truth of the body exposed. Not *fear* but a *Record of a Living Being.*

Madame D. is a latter-day Nakajima Kiichi.

Her recess is equivalent to the old man's window: the contour of an *actual* document[11] become illegible in the blinding light of the body's twin conscience and consciousness, resiliated under fervent dictatorship.

As for us, we are her bystanders.

(April 2015)

---

11. "...le document était toujours traité comme le langage d'une voix maintenant réduite au silence, —sa trace fragile, mais par chance déchiffrable." Michel Foucault. (...*the document was always treated as the language of a voice now reduced to silence, —its trace fragile, but by chance decipherable.*)

"Plus **the** swinging of the door"

←←← *Marassa - Dossou - Dossa* →→→

The figure four is as the four of the cross-roads plus the swinging of the door, which is the point itself of crossing, the moment of arrival and departure.

MAYA DEREN

Rapjazz by Frankétienne

Written in eponymous strains of rap and jazz, *Rapjazz* is Haitian writer and artist Frankétienne's coarsely voluptuous elegy to the city of Port-au-Prince. An inter- and intra-lingual "diary of a pariah," it chants the spoils of the city in the figure of the author's double "Foukifoura."[1]

Following closely after *Voix marassas* (1988), in which the author deploys the high powers of twinned genders

---

1. Foukifoura is the crossbred name of a figure later borrowed from *Rapjazz* into the play, *Foukifoura* (2000) and arising out of the coupling of Kreyòl and French that associates folly, or madness (*Fou*) with sexual play (*fourrer*) in the simple past (*foura*) conjoined by the Kreyòl for who (ki), thus: *fou-ki-foura*.

Furthering the enmeshment of madnesses through translingual referents, the narrator of *Rapjazz* is later self-described as *loco*—mad, in Spanish, but also the name attributed to a loa that is the guardian of sanctuaries, and especially the loa of vegetation; he is the one who confers to the leaves of trees their magical properties. Loco (alternately spelled Loko) is a personification of plants, and *cannot be identified to only two elements*. (My emphasis; mythologica.fr). According to Maya Deren, Loco also governs the principle of androgeneity (*Divine Horsemen*, 81). From the text: *Loco my burning sex the color of a watermelon heart tasting like moon syrup in the ass / of my envexed city of fornicating winds, of hodgepodge, of debris, of waste, of trash, of passions, of lies, of distress, of ravaging killings, of useless settings, of morbid atrocities, of heat and blood. // Loco for a rutting city with its coital smell. // Loco for a spitting city, pissing, sweating, bleeding. // Loco for a bruised / labored / sacked / rent city. // Loco for a city of cinders and obscure light. // Loco for a city that moves between living and dying.*

embodied by the figure of the Marassa—a power greater even than the Loas (spirits of Vodun) and capable of good or evil—*Rapjazz* (1989) pursues and heightens the inquest inscribed in the androgynous trope. Exemplified by the adjacency, and cross-contamination, of Kreyòl and French in the text, this trope denounces an idea of impermeability, be it of languages, bodies or nations, all of which are damningly and intractably historical. All are vulnerable not only to their defeat but to the violences that threaten to destroy them—the desegregation of particularities is conjoined to the quakes that lead both languages to collide with one another, in order to wrench from them a historical narrative that owes its voice to a shriek and its body to the banishment and defiance of its death.

By invoking memory against its obliviation, Frankétienne takes Port-au-Prince as his witness to (and evidence of) a present of trespass by extending the call of his text into an as-yet unaccounted for future, the parameters of which have not yet been set. In order to do so, he takes his double, 'Foukifoura' to task, and sets him(self) up as both madman and jester:

> Artistic creation, especially when it testifies to the difficulty of living, to existential discomfort and destructive barbarity, inscribes itself absolutely in the refusal of amnesia and death.
> Writing is my ultimate oasis in the fire of my deserts. My last port of registry on the tormented shores of this fabulous continent that is Life. My rapjazz of folly. (*Rapjazz*, p. 12)

Port-au-Prince is of course the capital of Haiti, the country that withstood Napoléon's incursions in 1802, resisting the reinstatement of slavery as it was genocidally re-implemented against the express (and unfulfilled) ideals of the French Revolution, in other existing colonies—though not without similarly fierce resistance.[2] Under the leadership of Toussaint Louverture, Haiti was the first independent post-colonial state to liberate itself from the French empire,[3] a distinction that nonetheless did not prevent the country from succumbing to countless political terrorisms, often abetted by Western powers, in the form of ruthless dictatorships, from Faustin Soulouque (president then emperor from 1847-59) to the Duvaliers (father and son, so-called "life-presidents," respectively from 1964-71 and 1971-86) and beyond, and under the repressive police forces of the *zinglins* of the 1800s, precursors of the tontons-macoutes of recent terrible memory.[4] Not to mention the burden of a ravaging AIDS epidemic and natural in addition to political disasters of recent years (including the 2010 earthquake that plundered the country) aggravated by the oversights and malpractices of humanitarian aid groups.[5]

---

2. See, in this vein, *La Mulâtresse Solitude* by André Schwarz-Bart (1972), a fictionalized account of the legendary figure of the Guadeloupean maroon, Solitude, who led a rebellion against the French forces, which culminated in the suicidal revolt of some 300 Guadeloupeans resisting re-enslavement. Solitude, who was captured, was hanged after a period of imprisonment during which time her pregnancy was brought to term. In English as *A Woman Named Solitude*, tr. Ralph Manheim. Syracuse University Press. Syracuse (NY), 2001.

3. Indeed, it was "the first black republic in the world." Jean-Claude Charles, *De si jolies petites plages*. Éditions Mémoire d'encrier. Montréal, 2016 [1982] (12).

4. The role of the *zinglins*, a secret police corps created by Haitian president, Faustin Soulouque (1782-1867), was to identify real, potential or imaginary enemies of the president and to eliminate them. *Zinglin*, alternately spelled *zenglen*, also signifies broken glass.

5. Several recent examples include: the U.N.'s introduction in 2010 of a cholera epidemic through poor sanitation practices; the downplayed rape of girls by any number of a hundred U.N. soldiers hurriedly repatriated to Sri Lanka; the I.M.F.'s abolishment of tariffs in the 1990s resulting in the devastation of Haiti's agriculture.

What *Rapjazz* achieves, in the continuance of Franketienne's extensive body of work, is nothing less than a revaluation of Haitian history in the figure of the city. It is, in a sense, a letter of a violent, defiled love, to Port-au-Prince. Unlike many of his contemporaries who exited the country under the Duvalier regimes, Franketienne, an interior exile, remained and founded a school in his neighborhood.[6] He developed an oblique form of resistance to the dictatorship in his writing through the experiential conjugation of Kreyòl with French.[7]

Nominal Corollaries

In the early 1970's Franketienne founded the *Spiralisme* movement with writers Jean-Claude Fignolé and René Philoctète.[8] While the proponents of *Le Spiralisme*, inspired in part by the Nouveau Roman and James Joyce, were fittingly unable to arrive at a consensual definition of the movement, in an interview with the journal *Dérives* Franketienne describes it as "a method of approach to try to seize reality that is always in movement."[9] A movement verging on dissolute forms, in which the writer is "condemned to eat his own book, leaf by leaf."[10]

---

6. Franketienne prefers to consider himself "miracled" rather than a "visionary" as a result of having lived through the Duvalier regime without having been tortured or imprisoned. This expression is inscribed in the 2004 work, *Miraculeuse*.
7. See Serge Martin, "Franketienne: Un Ultravocal" in *Voix et Relation*, 06/03/2014.
8. See Kaiama L. Glover's *Haiti Unbound: A Spiralist Challenge to the Postcolonialist Cannon*. Liverpool University Press. Liverpool, 2011.
9. Saint-John Kauss. "Le spiralisme de Franketienne," in *Potomitan*, 2007.
10. Franketienne. *L'Oiseau schizophone*. Éditions des Antilles. Port-au-Prince, 1993.

This same incompletable movement is at work in Franké-tienne's signature. Agglutinating two of his given names, Franck and Étienne, the author arrived at a Franketienne with multiple orthographies, each of which is respectively reflective of evolutions in the attested orthography of Haitian Creole (Kreyòl) in accordance with three periods: thus Franketienne reflects the author's signature in the 1970's; in the 1980's, in keeping with the contemporary convention of the time, the acute accent is dropped, leaving Franketienne; and then, reflecting the current spelling system for Haitian Kreyòl, Franketyèn.[11] Eventually, the name spiralled back, with its author, to Franketienne, the spelling adopted here.

Franketienne's engagement with the relationship between his two languages is essential to the frank politics of his work, and *Rapjazz* is an exemplar of this collision and the collusion between the two. It then goes without saying that *Rapjazz* imposes upon its translation into English strategies that arise directly from its structure, not the least of which is its distribution between and among two languages that inter-speak.

A Marassa Textimonial

The following reflections are to be placed under the sign of the Marassa—with the caution that this is thought that is still experimenting with itself, at times with some embarrassment, and so what will be glimpsed, in a manner of speaking, through a crack in the door, is me fingering something I am not sure how to touch—an intellectual experiment, in other words, which implicates the whole

---

11. Rachel Douglas. *Franketienne and Rewriting*. A Work in Progress. Lexington Books. Plymouth (UK), 2009 (vii-viii).

split body without aspiring to anything remotely conclusive. Every translative act risks, of necessity, a form of double exposure, of both translator and text. Here, it is not so much the Marassa figure in Franketienne's text that demands attention, as the text itself as a figure of the Marassa.

In chapter five of *Divine Horsemen*, Maya Deren's 1953 document on Haitian deities and Vodun, entitled "The Marassa—Two and Two Equals Five," Deren reveals the extent to which the Marassa is not the sum of its own parts. Elsewhere I have similarly proposed equivocation as a way of understanding translation against the tendency to seek in it something of a mathematical equation. In other words, "equals doesn't equal equals."[12]

Deren articulates it much more specifically: "Ghede, loa of life and death, is the corpse of the first man, who, in his original twinned nature, can be thought of as a cosmic totality segmented by the horizontal axis of the mirror divide into identical twins. The worship of the Marassa, the Divine Twins, is a celebration of man's twinned nature: half matter, half metaphysical; half mortal, half immortal; half human, half divine." The Marassa, Deren explains, are "the first humans, they are also the first, the original Dead." She later goes on to qualify what appears to figure itself as a binary: "The Haitian myth," she writes "has gone beyond the concept of Marassa of the same sex, as metaphysical reflection, and the Marassa of opposite sexes, as progenitive differentiation. [...] The Twins are not to be separated into competitive, conflicting dualism. In Voudoun one *and* one make three; two *and* two make five; for the *and* of the equation is the

12. "Postscript: A Short Film on Fascism," in *Asclepias: The Milkweeds*. Nightboat Books. New York, 2015 (149).

third and fifth part, respectively, the relationship which makes all the parts meaning."[13]

The Marassa, if one were to imagine a correlative in western thought might tender itself toward a third sex that isn't yet named (by Monique Wittig) a lesbian.[14] But a third sex that is yet unfixed in language and in sex, a sex into which one is not *forcibly* born, and that is not clamped to a seemingly intractable binary.

When Frankétienne writes in French and Kreyòl, as he does in *Rapjazz* and in other texts, part of the work he achieves is the dismantling of a linear understanding of translation as movement between two languages, or as might be figured by the meeting of two bodies (whatever their attributed sexes). What appear to be blocks of texts in differentiable languages reveal themselves to not simply mirror one another, as Deren suggests of the Marassa, but to refract and resorb one another; the languages devour each other, and their compost— Frankétienne's text—carries embedded trace elements that make their precise differentiation impracticable. Here, there is much to be said about the identification of the species and the Enlightened tendency to name, categorize, sequester, distinguish, isolate, discipline, quarantine, diagnose, measure, prognosticate, exile or evacuate. But perhaps some other time.

Take the following fairly economical example, from an earlier passage in *Rapjazz* in which Frankétienne writes: *Je brûle, je boule, je bouboule.*

13. Maya Deren. *Divine Horsemen: The Living Gods of Haiti*. McPherson and Company. Kingston (NY), 1953 (38-41).
14. "On ne naît pas femme," in *Questions féministes*, No. 8 (May 1980, 75-84). In English as "One is not born a woman," in *The Straight Mind and Other Essays*, 1981.

At first glance, French provides an expedient conduit for this sentence, and without attending to the reiterative alliteration, one could thrust oneself into *I burn, I roll, I hoot* (like an owl). But the surface impression in this instance, as it often is, is misleading. A closer reading of the clause reveals an internal translation at work in the line, into which Frankétienne has smuggled Kreyòl elements that *appear* as French elements, producing inter-, intra- and translingual polysemy.[15] *Je brûle*: I burn. *Je boule*: I burn. Because *boule* in Kreyòl means to burn.[16] The second clause surreptitiously translates the first, as itself. And *bouboule*, a double-burn in a sense, deploys the twinning translation for the sheer pleasure of its sonority. English can offer up a paltry *booboo*, not a hoot, but a whimper. To return for a moment to the middle clause, *je boule*, Patwah's fortuitous (for this translation) term for *burn* is *bun*.[17] A happy coincidence here retains the French sense of the roll. Thus: *I burn, I bun, I booboo*.

A last note before casting off, without having attended to the anthropophagic valence of Frankétienne's work, an impetus that situates it very powerfully in the Americas, along the central axis of which the island of Hispaniola is split, and which is perceivable as intertwined by the hermaphroditic

---

15. Not to mention various degrees of disguise. One could push further into imagining this text as a marauder, indeed, a suspect and not altogether traceable figure apprehending the shores of an unfixed littoral under cover of night.

16. "Par contre, il omet beaucoup de mots fondamentaux comme bouler pour brûler..." (*On the other hand, he omits many fundamental words like bouler for burn...*) Pradel Pompilus. *Le problème linguistique häïtien.* Éditions Fardin. Port-au-Prince, 1985 (97).

17. The Patwah expression *bun them*, which intends to mean "bothers them," literally translates as "burns them." The Rastafarian expression *fiyah bun* (fire burn) is an expression used to strongly denounce something or someone. See *Jamaican Patwah: Patois and Slang Dictionary*.

trinity ("*I eat myself interminably / my shadow and I / unbearable Siamese in precincts forbidden to my musical saw.*"[18]). In Haiti, when asked the simple question *Sak pase?*,[19] a possible answer, in the everyday, under the archipelago's sun, is *N'ap boule.*[20] I burn.

The ontological fires are the same that ignite the author's desire to consume and to consummate himself in the city's severally sexed conflagration. It was Sappho, in a fragment, who may have written, *you burn me.*[21] To which echo, perhaps, Frankétienne's therianthropic reply might be: "*To the beating of dusk raising the great fires of prestige and prestidigitation, my fingers light up virtuosos. / The sun awakens. The wind slides slowly over my nocturnal burns. I leaf through my scales, my buds and my flowers. I file away my scores, my petals and my words. // To the vice of writing / for me silence is fatal.*"

(January & November, 2015)

---

18. From *Rapjazz*. Éditions Spirale. Port-au-Prince, 1989.

19. *How are you?*

20. I am grateful to Rodney Saint-Éloi for such elucidations as this.

21. A mis-translation, if one is to believe Anne Carson, and one she purposefully retains in her translations of Sappho's fragments, for the sheer impression upon her memory. *If not, Winter: Fragments of Sappho*. Knopf. New York, 2002 (77).

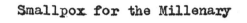

Smallpox for the Millenary

La guerre ne l'avait pas rendu intact à la vie.

LÉON WERTH

During the War to end War, some time between the Baskervilles and Agent Orange, there was the small matter of a typhoid outbreak among field soldiers that the French war ministry sought to control through the enforcement of a vaccine. The risks of the epidemic were matched by the risks to which soldiers were exposed by this experimental inoculation, and so with the gangrenous trenches, and the steady threat of ballistics, the internal matter of the body's hygiene was a further front on which to defend oneself. None of which was received without some form of resistance, and nor could any claim immunity. So the soldiers defended their bodies, just as they defended against their bodies, and as is the case in and outside of great works of literature, with varying degrees of reprisal, punitive measures, and success, leading, at times to the great catch-all: death. The edicts and decrees of course assume the form of national dictates, subsuming the one into the many, and abrogating, thereby, the necessity for, or the right to, autonomy. It is no secret that battlefields are the experimental grounds of chemical catastrophe, biological assault, and what are often referred to as medical advancements. Mustard gas and blood transfusions provide two apparently tidy examples. Never mind that the swamps doused with Napalm still carry their burn, or that the birds stifled their song at Birkenau. Nor that, generally speaking, war itself is a great ground of merciless trials carried out against populations, civilian or otherwise. "As you are about to leave, you say that you aren't vaccinated against typhoid and you burn your record and you say: 'When I was asked whether I was vaccinated, I thought that it was for smallpox.' You're given eight days in the slammer, but you've got a month to go." (Léon Werth). For the soldier cuckolded by the state, it is a kind of sentencing, and in either case, whatever the military's position, "the army" as Kaji scances in Kobayashi Masaki's *Ningen no jōken* (in English as *The Human Condition*), "is the enemy."

Alain Jugnon's *a body, in spite* may have nothing to do with any of the above. But between eight days and a month, there is enormous room for error. And the question might arise as to which side of the bars will constitute the proving ground. Even admitting that the bars have symbolic value, and that *nothing to do* is precisely where one is mobilized. As Jugnon's text declaims: "It is of public notoriety that nothing." Provided, of course, that one is able to know "who is one."

à corps défendant names the exact tension between a body in action and a body's inaction. And translation here is most magnanimously of no help in elucidating the torqued idiomatic expression that has expunged the reflexivity of *à son corps défendant*, for which English offers as a literal equivalent *the resistance to an attack* while expressing idiomatic *regret*. The coexistence of these two contrary efforts in this locution prepare the ground for a battlefield of philosophical ailment and semantic reprisal, the gauge for which abandons the usual referents. The result, for the English language reader, is a rageful distance from an identifiable torment. Just as the war is subsumed into its obliquity, the language of the war is full of faces "visible on the bedsheet." But isn't history, too, a concatenation of street names and dwellings, more or less flung open to public view, and swept into "the wind passing through." Lineage is a form of melancholy made of finished philosophies. For José Ortega y Gasset, "even before entering the fray, [man] already carries a wound in his temple." He means time. And if the time of translation abounds in this kind of belatedness, it is made more pressing by the kind of present that is at stake in *a body, in spite*. Jugnon takes the man with his wound and declares him to be alive: "It was always known and yet, all life long, it will only ever be a matter of that."

In his essay, *Athéologiques*, the author provides what may be this text's loophole: "The name poses its dead: the name shows contempt to the living by saying clearly and distinctly the infinite individuation, the theatre of permanent death, which is all life and which is all thought." It is a long march from France's inroads of 1940 to becoming "the son of one's own events" (Gilles Deleuze). The "philosopher-body," such as it is contended by Jugnon, is a porous fortification, and if the hole widens inward, it is because its greatest capacity is also its most visibly hidden.

Having now crossed the Atlantic into this English of the Americas, *a body, in spite* will have other smallpoxes to contend with. Against the ripest forms of violence in the guise of cultivated amnesia, and fascisms of the everyday, Jugnon's work reminds history of its regimens, and the present of its pettiest details. It is against the erasure of these details that Alain Jugnon places these words back in the entrails of the body, where the mouth is summoned to its defenses.

(January 2017)

Epigraph:

Werth: War had not returned him intact to life.

Works cited:

Léon Werth. *Clavel chez les majors*. Viviane Hamy. Paris, 2006 (1918).

Alain Jugnon. *Athéologiques. L'humanisme, le communisme et Charles Péguy.* Dasein Éditions. Millery, 2016.

Kobayashi Masaki, dir. *Ningen no jōken [The Human Condition]*. Shochiku, 1959-1961.

José Ortega y Gasset. "Miseria y esplendor de la traducción," 1937. In English as "The Misery and the Splendor of Translation," tr. E.G. Miller, in *Theories of Translation*, eds. Rainer Schulte and John Biguenet. University of Chicago Press. Chicago, 1992 (93-112).

The Solitary Deaths of Mizoguchi Kenji

Make away.

If I stop at a single sentence as at an image, emptying the page of its signs having suddenly become superfluous, or else propelling themselves like a current, displacing the exact frame of a philosophical convention, what is given, to me as to anyone, and in any case abducts and assigns me, in the manner of a dream, sometimes terrifically, and having arisen in a film, where, in the position of the only spectator, which is to say multiply, I become the mute witness, not by choice and therefore incidentally, and as a result *by accident*, and reel by reel, of the *solitary deaths of Mizoguchi Kenji*, such as they arise in the thinking of Gilles Deleuze, suspended between the eddies of otherwise rhetoric, the seizure of movement, its temporality, whereas it falls under the purview of no language, ultimately, the desire to say so, nor the name of the filmmaker, it is the words themselves detached from the density of a cine-philosophy,[1] as of an unverifiable truth, in other words driven by what it is given to see, without in fact wanting to do so, and in the margins of its own limits. The "solitary deaths" of Mizoguchi are females, all, and without a doubt, it is not enough to enumerate them, nor to catalogue the films fallen from the history of cinema, including the castaways, bodiless and named, to each his grave, the late cinema, from film to fire, starting at the insolite, and already much discussed, post-war image of an impotent goddess of

---

1. Gilles Deleuze. *L'image-mouvement.* Minuit. Paris, 1983 (265).

christianity, abandoned to her shame, and looking down from her stone tower in the stomach of the ruined church, and by the dulled brilliance of its devitrified stain, onto the square where the night women are warring, *a posteriori*, under a voiceless icon and so with nothing more than a syphilitic promise that rejects the occidental prayer implanted in Ōsaka, a presumptuous compassion, but human matter reduced to its voluminous dust.[2] If, as the filmmaker affirms in his work notes, "emotion is needed, not a commentary,"[3] one must question the aptness of verbiage intent on circumscribing the mechanism calling for flight, into the netting of language, the senses in question, the sequence shot of scarcely a thought because reduced to the silence by which it unravels. This silence, made plural, bears name of city and body of sector, from Kyōto to Ōsaka, and from Gion to Shinsekai, exfoliating the eras as the ages, from Heian to Showa, and lingering over Meiji. The "solitary deaths"[4] of Mizoguchi Kenji are females, all, and each dies in the eye of the cinema, under the invisible hands of convention, and in the flames of loves betrayed by their armatures, in other words the sensible stare of the filmmaker, turned over under a fragile lid, the mists of the fogged film strip. The concentric circles descend, infernal, from lowliness to lowliness, effacing themselves as assiduously as they are produced, the body as much as the face, abandoned to the grating city or the deported song of a mother or a lover. As much as these names are posthumously conceded to the screen scanning their solitude, the individual

---

2. Mizoguchi Kenji, dir. *Yoru no onna tachi* [*Women of the Night*]. Shochiku, 1948.

3. Mizoguchi Kenji as quoted in Yoda Yoshikata, *Souvenirs de Kenji Mizoguchi*, tr. Koichi Yamada, et al. Cahiers du Cinéma. Paris, 1997 (107).

4. The published English-language translation of *L'image-mouvement* renders "mort solitaire" as "lonely death" (196). Gilles Deleuze, *Cinema I, The Movement-Image*, tr. Hugh Tomlinson and Barbara Habberjam. The Athlone Press. London, 1986 [1983].

subjects of the cinematic narratives prove themselves to be isolated inside the swell of history, an inexorable detainment as given affliction. Because *death*, without fail, is a sort of murder, decanted in time, whose foil is a devastated permanence (that of war and prostitution, conjugal or illicit). The final gaze carried over the reeds to the end of Oyū-sama,[5] committed against her own person, bespeaks the absolute limit of a subjectivity that reveals itself to be absence of a possible limit, and renunciation of succession, of all intimate bonds with the world such as it is refused her. World without I to which the filmmaker bequeaths himself in aparté at the approach of the philosopher, giving resonance to the lines of Sōseki Natsume when, at the death of a friend, he writes:

> Those chrysanthemums
> That you find, cast them all down
> In the coffin deep[6]

In Mizoguchi there is no coffin, but a hollow world, doubled over on the riverbanks, at the edge of a shallow island, or an untraversable road, and even when its reach extends beyond a funerary mound, the gaze past an avowable lie, the body, weighted, loses face and the present can only resorb itself in time. Notably when the last shot joins the first, to the point of irrecognizability, for not being *the same*.[7] The horizon is an ache, and its vertigo evinces a vertical incompletion, free fall of a statufied vision,[8] a pall made ever more appalling for its obstinacy.[9]

---

5. Mizoguchi Kenji, dir. *Oyū-sama* [*Miss Oyu*]. Daiei Film, 1951.

6. Sōseki Natsume. *Inside my glass doors*, tr. Sammy L. Tsunematsu. Tuttle. North Clarendon (VT), 2002. These lines are dedicated to *keishū* writer Ōtsuka Kusuo (1875-1910). An essayist, poet and fiction writer, she was the author of *Sora daki* (*Incense burner*).

7. Mizoguchi Kenji, dir. *Ugetsu monogatarai* [*Ugetsu*]. Daiei Film, 1953.

8. Mizoguchi Kenji, dir. *Yōkihi* [*Princess Yang Kwang-Fei*]. 1955.

9. Mizoguchi Kenji, dir. *Tōkyō kōshinkyoku* [*Tokyo March*]. 929.

During an interview granted after the death of the filmmaker by screenwriter Yoda Yoshikata, the latter interprets a calligraphy written in Mizoguchi's hand:

> You see, this *tense* (calligraphy) is comprised of four characters, the first of which is simply the drawing of an eye. The four together signify 'With each new look, one must wash one's eyes.' …[10]

Mizoguchi's mortuary mask was donated to Henri Langlois, and is today among the archives of the Cinémathèque française at Bercy. The mask, congealed skin, not only of the face of the filmmaker, but effigy of his own "solitary death," consolidates the concatenation of demises dissolved in his films, into the mute absorption of Anju,[11] silenced to save her brother Zushio, sinking in the exact place where the extinguished voice of the philosopher waits. How does the gaze assume the form of what it sees itself beseeching. If all of these deaths, said to be solitary, captured only to be evacuated, cast themselves each individually onto a female body without an actual world, one must believe, with Mizoguchi, placed under the eye of Deleuze, in their declension for all time, in the feminine. Whereas the impossibility of seeing and the reversal of the knowledge upon which this thinking rests. The "solitary deaths" of Mizoguchi Kenji under the ensign Gilles Deleuze are nothing other than the self-less appeal to the transgendered world having fled the body thus designated.

(August 2017 - May 2018)

---

10. « Yoda Yoshikata et Miyagawa Kazuo, » in *Mizoguchi Kenji. Cahiers du cinéma*, hors série, September 1978 (22).

11. Mizoguchi Kenji, dir. *Sanshō Dayū* [*Sansho the Bailiff*]. Daiei Film, 1954.

(A)versions — a
deliberative dossier

Read what is written out; address what is disqualified from speaking; hold two words in one mouth split along a single seam and ask nothing. The unreachable interiority of the mortuary impression cannot be cast upon any face. And the duplications on which forensics rely, whether in the diagnostic of dictatorships or of artworks, can only bespeak amassment, and evacuation. // At the close of L'homme révolté, *Albert Camus evokes Ernst Dwinger's diary of Siberia, published in French as* La mort en Pologne, *in which the author evokes an imprisoned German lieutenant, having built for himself a silent piano made of wooden keys. "There," Camus writes, "in the overcrowded misery, in the midst of a ragged throng, he composed a strange music that he alone could hear." I will not, with Camus, go so far as to speak here of human grandeur; but I will answer to the bruised border between fragility and its most confidential defence.*

These words were intended as a conclusion to the first of the three texts gathered in this dossier. Here, unburdened of their context, they make a promise that is predicated on breaking.

"Who were the bodies?" asks Colonel Ted Lawson, interpreted by Richard Widmark in Stanley Kramer's *Judgment at Nuremberg* (1961). This alone may encompass the question posed by literature, and certainly that posed by the texts herein. Its ontology is tragically objected, and its object-hood belied precisely by its reach for nomination. Neither is achievable, and no law will succeed in delivering *the bodies* from their abjection, nor the appeal for a name. Perhaps it is for this reason alone—having written these texts under the eye of an ever incontinent Law (but which Law, for there are several)—that their writing would prove ever incomplete (incompletable), and the accumulation of versions, and repetition of certain historical parameters, with careful adjustment, prove necessary for the state of *sideration* in which the writer finds herself and her text. Something in the *matter* of this inquiry continues to elude me. It may simply be in the reversal of histories, a sudden collapse (but it isn't sudden at all) into a time given to scrutiny, which arises again and again as an insoluble present, rejected by the sort of reasoning that arrived there in the first place. (The first place is always taken: this is its tragedy, and its lure—the bull in the ring knows it, pierced, as it is with spears, and choking on barbiturates, as does the sora in the marsh eyeing the gun, and this knowledge does nothing to quell the killing jeers nor repeal the laws founded in dictature and upheld in states of condemnable innocence).

The decision to include three of the existing versions of this text in this dossier may be convergent with the sorts of repetitions present in the cinema of Kobayashi Masaki—most notably the recurrence of footage of Sugamo Prison across thirty years of filmmaking, and the return to the question of War, its indecency, and the human willingness to be corrupted. If "the end of the world has [indeed] already ended" (Pasolini) then we are choking on it, and the question must be raised again and again as to this end and the ways in which it has been written, and in which it continues to be written out. In this sense, the testimony becomes as suspect as the confession, when it finds itself incarcerated in juridical structures the violence of which is persistently reinforced against the liberties it claims to defend. If ever the door proved itself to be a wall, now is that time.

What follows, then, are three texts: the first, "We give our lives for nothing," borrows its title from a 1971 film by Kobayashi Masaki—*Inochi bo ni furo*—perplexingly released in English as "Inn of Evil." It was the text accompanying a screening of *Habe atsuki heya* (*The Thick-Walled Room*, 1956 [1953]), and read at the School of the Art Institute of Chicago in June 2017 as part of a two-day film seminar entitled ", to the shadow a shadow" (language borrowed from Ingeborg Bachmann).

The following December, at Spertus Institute, excerpts from the same film were shown, and an adjusted version of the text, here included as "The Open, Under Cover," was read as a prelude to a public conversation with the painter Matthew Girson.

Finally, "Alula, for posterity" was the interstitial text of a lecture given at Glendon College in Toronto, in November, and preceded by an excerpt from *India Song* (the film/text) by Marguerite Duras. It inscribes in its form serious departures from the initial writings.

Because no finality is final, Alula is followed by a brief text which introduces the French writing of Alula, and which was read at the Centre Anne-Hébert at Université Sherbooke (Québec), also in November.

Whether these texts are to be apprehended as rehearsals (*répétitions*) or as reinforcements against obvious disaggregation is not immediately evident. What is more certain is that the art gallery in which one is given to speak may well prove, beneath its controlled surfaces, to share an intention with the shooting gallery: that of capture and elimination (because exhibition implies *seizure*). Such that the accrual of versions can only signify a form of *fraying*, and their assemblage here must be indicative, not just of the impossibility of reconstruction, but of a caution against such aspirations.

La rupture du rapport est ici le rapport. - Jacques Derrida

"We give our lives for nothing."

We see ourselves in projection, and behold
the city, in one of its poor naked hours,
terrifying as each nudity.
A scorched earth whose blaze,
extinguished this evening or millennia ago,
is an infinite circle of pink ruins,
whitening coals and bones, scaffoldings
washed away by rain and then burnt
by a new sun. [...]
     Maybe the Bomb
has gone off without my knowing.
Yes, that must certainly be it. And the end
of the World has already happened: a thing
mute, fallen into the counterlight of dusk.
Shadow, who is working in this era.

PIER PAOLO PASOLINI (1962)
tr. N. + J. Scappettone

In a 1966 essay Pier Paolo Pasolini asks: "Now what is a presence? it is ... it is something which speaks for itself. ... It is a language. *Reality is a language.*"

"Cinema," he affirms, "is the written language of this reality as language." (133)

The reflexivity evoked by Pasolini, the *thing speaking for itself,* is predicated, not only, upon a polysemous proclivity—in other words, a tendency toward a distribution of meanings not limited to a single significance—but on a form of doubling that recuses repetition. Not only is *the written language of this reality as language* doubled over itself, but it literally overtakes itself, following one of the French senses of the verb *doubler. Doubler*: to overtake, as in a speeding car on a road veering off the face of a cliff, or an emotion too great to withstand. In either case there is a loss of coordinates, a concerted effort of resistance to a force greater than either gravity or torpor and that potentially produces vertigo or collapse. In this instance, only time is slow, because it is intractable.
Doubled over, in other words: not repeatable.

In a later essay, this time from 1971, Pasolini further proposes "that reality is a language, and also in real life, as pragmatic dialogue between us and things (including our body)." The enigmatic quality of "almost everything" lies in its potential to be polysemic. (258) A polysemy which is imaginable as a form of fracture, a permanent and continuous displacement of sense along discontinuous lines that produce an infinite number of limits, each of which asks to be named, and so transgressed, such that in return, the temporality of presence is denied the present out of which it claims, semantically, to be made. "The arts," wrote Sōseki Natsume in 1915, in the year preceding his death, "are not born in the world of the Same. Even admitting that they take root there, it is only once they have entered the world of the Multiple that they finally flourish." Any attempt to bring them back to an originary past reveals in its place "an absolute void" (94-95).

In other words: *presence*, amplified, as it is, by the voice it assigns itself, loses itself as reference, of necessity, in order to achieve the commission of *reality*, its summons. Which is precisely where it topples into fiction, a fiction made more severe, more grave, and more defiantly acute, and potentially murderous, than the *real* against which it is often so misguidedly measured.

A breach made of breaches and comprised of just as many embrasures. The exact and incalculable distance between precedence and belatedness. Between a body and its disappearance; between a name and its destruction; between a war and its accounting. A ghost become apparent.

What is *the thing* then?

On April 18, 1942, the U.S. carried out its first air raid over Japan. According to historian and literary scholar Donald Keene, sixteen medium-range bombers "dropped bombs on what the United States officially described as military targets in Tokyo. [...] The photographs of their accomplishments prove only that they sank a small fishing boat." (21)

Reading Walter Benjamin, Jacques Derrida, in *Force de loi*, proposes that "a body is never present for itself, for what it is. It appears while disappearing or while making what it represents disappear: one for the other." (102) Or, in the words leant to Tamura in *Nobi* (in English as *Fires on the Plain*) by Ōoka Shōhei—like Kobayashi Masaki, a Pacifist, and serviceman conscripted into Japan's Greater East Asia War: "It was not because I was still alive that I clung to the notion of life, but because I was already dead."

The estimated exchange value is perennially posthumous. The present is ever indebted to itself. It is its own archive, and subject to the same kinds of depredations as are the artefacts of war, with particular attention given to the large numbers of missing documents, not to mention the bodies, searched for with equal desperation, as though one were somehow equivalent to the other, with each concealing a hidden script, and in any case, *evidence* of the mutilated forms by which existence must now excuse itself. There are since Pinochet the masked shards of bone drying in the inextinguishable sun of the Atacama desert, which has been sifted through for decades by the hands of surviving elders; the manuscripts buried by Sonderkommando in the soil of Auschwitz-Birkenau, whose dispersal, and likely pillage or disintegration, is unrecoverable; the stacks of mildewed photographs and extracted confessions at Tuol Sleng Prison in Cambodia, among which a known image of an execution remains yet to be found by its filmmaker; and the hundreds of thousands of pages of documented atrocities, including the biological experiments carried out by Units 731 and 100—equal to those undertaken by Mengele at Auschwitz—, burned by the Japanese military between the declaration of unconditional surrender on August 15th, 1945 and the arrival of the U.S. occupying forces two weeks later. Some 70% of existing documents by historical accounts. Exceptions that confirm the rule of slaughter, the hyper-extension of realities, and the ideological insistence of execution: the execution of orders, the execution of prisoners, the execution of tasks carried out to the impeccable point of exhaustion. The capital punishment of humanity.

To speak of war crimes is of course a redundancy.

It was several decades after the end of Japan's Greater East Asia War before Kobayashi Masaki undertook to produce his documentary *Tokyo Saiban*. Released in 1983, the four-and-a half-hour film is extracted from thirty thousand reels of the proceedings of the International Military Tribunal for the Far-East (IMTFE), otherwise known as the Tokyo Trial. The film opens with an image of a Nazi insignia crashing in slow motion onto the ground from atop the lintel of an official German building, signifying the fall of fascism and the end of the European war. It follows in meticulous detail the court proceedings, registering its protocolar tedium, quietly exposing its inherent patronism and serious breaches resulting from mis-translation and at times, for the sake of expediency, a blatant lack of translation. Set against an able assemblage of archival images that double back in time in keeping with the incidents addressed by the trial, from various instances of Japanese imperialist war, in China, Burma and the Philippines, including the Bataan Death March and the Massacre of Nanjing, the Potsdam conference, the subsequent atomic blasts at Hiroshima and Nagasaki, and the U.S. nuclear tests over Bikini atoll, the film concludes with the iconic 1972 photograph by Nick Ut of a nine-year-old girl running naked from her village north-west of Saigon which had just "mistakenly" been doused in Napalm by the South Vietnamese air force. Throwing into question, not only war itself, and the images by which it is conveyed, but the *processes* by which its judgments are distributed, and far from attempting to exonerate criminals of war, it seeks instead to expose the crime of war itself and the logic by which it is performed, into and especially the contrived judicial procedures which oversee its outcomes. If *Tokyo Saiban* shares with John L. Ginn, U.S. serviceman and author of a monograph on Sugamo Prison, the grim conclusion that "When we evaluate the impact of World War II war crimes trials on reducing future atrocities, we must admit failure," (241) the film patiently draws out the extension of war into the meting out of punishment, and lack, precisely, on the part of the presiding judges of any kind of reflexivity. What can be viewed as a "lack of consciousness," following Jacques Derrida, still in *Force de Loi*, "does not arise by accident, nor the amnesia that follows. It is," he continues, "the very passage from presence to representation." As Benjamin laconically observes, there is something "rotten in law," (286) and it is this rot, with its firm roots in the violence by which the law finds its means and its basis, that places it in direct relation with the war it seeks to adjudicate, with its recourse to methods of aggression, including but not limited to the death penalty, for its vindication: in other words the violent assertion or the law itself.

> *For who would bear [...]*
> *Th' oppressor's wrong, the proud man's contumely*
> *The pangs of dispriz'd love, the law's delay,*
> *The insolence of office, and the spurns*
> *That merit of th' unworthy takes,*
> *When he himself might his quiētus make*
> *With a bare bodkin?*
> *(Hamlet, III, I, 70-76)*

Kabe Atsuki Heya—The Thick-Walled Room, also translatable as *Room with thick walls*—marks Kobayashi's first in a series of indictments against war, and the faulted record of human history, which will include the epic, six-part, *Ningen no jōken* (*The Human Condition*, 1959-1961, based on a bestselling novel by Gomikawa Junpei), and the exquisitely restrained *Seppuku* (released in English as *Hara-kiri*, 1962). *Kabe atsuki heya* was completed shortly after the nominal end of the U.S. occupation of Japan, not long after the Tokyo Trial's 27-month tenure, and during the entirety of which, indeed extending from 1945 into 1952, Japan was prohibited from any and all critical discussion of the atomic bombs, a tyrannical injunction with which the press complied. Less effective than its counterpart in Germany, the Nuremberg Trial, the Tokyo Trial, with its marked inequalities, was carried out in a theatre of equally careful execution of design. According to journalist Mark Gayn, in his *Japan Diary* (1948), not only was the courtroom, during its construction, "ripped up because it was felt that it did not live up to the importance of the occasion," (200-201) at its first session "all that was shown was a very large and photogenic room. Its relative unimportance was betrayed by the first act of inanity." (209) Gayn was likely referring to a moment when, in the dock, nationalist philosopher and spy, Okawa Shumei, who was later found to be suffering from tertiary syphillis, suddenly "leaned forward and hit [wartime prime minister] Tojo Hideki on the head with a rolled copy of the indictment."

By the time *Tokyo Saiban* is being prepared, Sugamo Prison, which is at the centre of the moment in history it addresses, has already been demolished. Its demonstration, as with any text, and still with Derrida "ruins under your eyes the distinctions it proposes. It exhibits and archives the very movement of its implosion, leaving in place what is referred to as a text, the phantom of a text which, itself in ruins, both foundation and conservation, arrives at neither one nor the other and remains there, up to a point, for a certain time, legible and illegible, like the exemplary ruin that warns us singularly as to the destiny of every other text and every other signature in their relation to the law, in other words necessarily, alas, to a certain police" (104).

Sugamo Prison, designed by the U.S. trained architect Yorinaka Tsumaki after several years of study in Germany, was officially opened in 1895. Constructed over a four-year period, the 'international' prison, destined to hold prisoners from the west, had a 1.6 km perimeter, which was encircled by a brick wall 5 metres high. Its main gate, 4 metres tall, was made of wood reinforced with iron. Inside the compound, two small watchtowers presided each over five large cell blocks designed to hold two thousand four hundred prisoners, with several housed to a cell. It was destroyed in 1971, and in its place, Japan's tallest residential shopping complex was erected. The memory of the prison's monumentality, of its architecture is imbued with "the precarious experience of its very fragility" (Derrida, 105).

So it is that two films, placed at either end of Kobayashi's career, converge on a single historical moment. Based on a screenplay by Abe Kōbō, *Kabe atsuki heya* draws not only from the notebooks of class B and C war criminals, but makes use of archival footage, extrapolating from the real the matter of its fiction; some of this footage will return in *Tokyo Saiban*, specifically that of Sugamo Prison, so that it functions not only as a memory of a recorded place, but the memory of that memory, belatedly inscribed on film. *The thing speaking for itself* in this instance, is not only the language that is reality conveyed as *cinema*, but the very architecture that seeks to delineate it. Its fragility is in its relation to the body it seeks to contain, a body in which the disaggregation of existing structures is evidenced—unlike the sentinel in Paul Virilio's Atlantikwall bunker, whose body espouses the rigidity of the concrete in which it is enclosed, engaging a sort of pre-emptive *rigor mortis*. The fossil, in this instance, to echo a title from a later film by Kobayashi, *Kaseki* (1974), dances into its dismemberment: a dismemberment upon which its freedom is predicated. If the prison house remains intractable in its construction, with its persuasive methods of enclosure, exclusion, and extinction by means of execution, it relies on methods of translation that are necessarily erroneous, if not fictive. And it is by means of these methods, that something of the *real* traverses the imposing limits with their gaping shadows, wounded light that succeeds eventually in loosening the structure from its certitudes, and introduces temporal and often untimely indistinctions that prove at times to be as fatal as the hammer blows delivered to stone. In any case they present themselves as more convincing in their arguments than the stark outlines of confinement to which they are subjected. This is as true for Hamada, whose criminal liberty is assured by his obsequious manipulations, as it is for Kawanishi for whom the walls become projectiles against which he can only throw himself. Here is where the prison structure reveals some of its insidious duplicitousness, folding and enfolding its own magnitude into its most intimate interstices.

Perhaps though, with Yoshikata's friend Ueda, and with a nod to Akinari's *Ugetsu*, we must ourselves acknowledge a degree of *madness*, to be able to sit still as spectators of these devouring shadows, and admit that the moon has indeed "come into the room," once and for all.

(June 25, 2017)

The Open, Under Cover

La rupture du rapport est ici le rapport.

JACQUES DERRIDA

Who were the bodies?

COL. TED LAWSON
Judgment at Nuremburg

The open, under cover

In a recent interview, when asked whether during the bombing of Nantes in WWII he had hidden "underground, in the cellars," Paul Virilio, replied, in French, of course: "There were gardens out back. We went there. We were afraid of being buried. We heard people shrieking in the caves, drowned by the water mains. So my father had said: we're not going. So we went into the gardens, we lay down on the ground."[1]

In the very free English-language re-writing of this published text, the word *jardins*—gardens—is supplanted by the word fields. The distance is intractable between these two designations. *Hay un jardín* writes Argentine poet Alejandra Pizarnik whose body is formulated by a same semblance of elsewhere that escapes language demonstrably, in which a garden seen, and uninhabited—*nadie está en algún jardín*—can suddenly transform itself into a field: a battlefield, a field of vision, a minefield, a cotton field, a radiation field, a killing field, in which the body takes place out of sight. In which its traversal is implied: standing, lying down. Under cover and in the open.

---

1. Caroline Dumoucel. "Un long entretien avec Paul Virilio," in *Vice* (24 septembre 2010). English translation by Pauline Eiferman, in *Vice* (September 2, 2010).

The photographer of the Atlantikwall bunkers at the close of the war also concerned himself with t he rigidification of the body of the sentinel overcome by the reinforced concrete circumscribing him, with, as his only viewpoint, that proffered by the loopholes. Those petrified ships, with walls three-metres thick, quickly threw themselves into the water after 1945, withheld by no durable bind that would have anchored them in time to the eventually friable ground. These were unfounded buildings. So they float in the sea, or sink into the sand, sideways. And their mariner is more akin to stone than to water.

Not repeatable

In a 1966 essay Pier Paolo Pasolini asks: "Now what is a presence? it is … it is something which speaks for itself. … It is a language. *Reality is a language.*"[2]

The reflexivity evoked by Pasolini, the *thing speaking for itself,* is predicated, not only, upon a polysemous disposition but on a form of doubling that recuses repetition. Not only is *the written language of this reality as language* doubled over itself, but it literally overtakes itself, following one of the French senses of the verb *doubler. Doubler*: to overtake, as in a speeding car on a road veering off the face of a cliff, or an emotion too great to withstand. In either case there is a loss of coordinates, a concerted effort of resistance to a force greater than either gravity or torpor and that potentially produces vertigo or collapse. In this instance, only time is slow, because it is intractable.
Doubled over, in other words: not repeatable.

---

2. Pier Paolo Pasolini, *Heretical Empiricism*, tr. Ben Lawton and Louise K. Barnett. New Academic Publishing. Washington (DC), 2005 [1998].

The commission of reality

In a later essay, this time from 1971, Pasolini further proposes "that reality is a language, [a] pragmatic dialogue between us and things (including our body)." The enigmatic quality of "almost everything" lies in its potential to be polysemic.[3] A polysemy which is imaginable as a form of fracture, a permanent and continuous displacement of sense along discontinuous lines that produce an infinite number of limits, each of which asks to be named, and so transgressed, such that in return, the temporality of presence is denied the present out of which it claims, semantically, to be made. "The arts," wrote Sōseki Natsume in 1915, in the year preceding his death, "are not born in the world of the Same. Even admitting that they take root there, it is only once they have entered the world of the Multiple that they finally flourish." Any attempt to bring them back to an originary past reveals in its place "an absolute void."[4]

In other words: *presence*, amplified, as it is, by the voice it assigns itself, loses itself as reference, in order to achieve the commission of *reality*, its summons. Which is precisely where it topples into fiction, a fiction made more severe, more grave, and more defiantly acute, and potentially murderous, than the *real* against which it is often so misguidedly measured.

A breach made of breaches and comprised of just as many embrasures. The exact and incalculable distance between precedence and belatedness. Between a body and its disappearance; between a name and its destruction; between a war and its accounting. A ghost become apparent.

---

3. *Heretical Empiricism*, *op. cit.*, 258.
4. This text is adapted from the French translation of *À travers la vitre* by Sōseki Natsume, tr. René de Ceccatty and Ryōji Nakamura. Payot & Rivages. Paris, 1993. (94-95)

Dead Already

In the dream that dreams me Kawanishi wakes up screaming. These are the hours preceding the improvised gallows at Sugamo, a now-demolished Tokyo prison that bore the name of a fibrous waterweed out of which paper can be wrought, or an ersatz of cotton, strong enough for hanging B-class war criminals, for whom the walls become projectiles against which they can only throw themselves. In Kobayashi Masaki's filmography, Sugamo Prison stands at either end of his production, between the U.S. occupation of Japan and *Gojira*'s double (1984), duplicated over the course of years, in a persistent investigation into the contemporary crime of war and its insidious adjudication. A rejection of clemency, despite the judgments handed down at Nuremberg and Tokyo, where the wests were one.

For example: On April 18, 1942, the U.S. carried out its first air raid over Japan. According to historian and literary scholar Donald Keene, sixteen medium-range bombers "dropped bombs on what the United States officially described as military targets in Tokyo. [...] The photographs of their accomplishments prove only that they sank a small fishing boat."[5]

The estimated exchange value is perennialy posthumous. The present is ever indebted to itself. It is its own archive, and subject to the same kind of depredations as are the artefacts of war, with particular attention given to the large numbers of missing documents, not to mention the bodies, searched for with equal desperation, as though one were somehow equivalent to the other, with each concealing a hidden script,

---

5. *So Lovely a Country Will Never Perish*. Columbia University Press. New York, 2010 (21).

and in any case, *evidence* of the mutilated forms by which existence must now recuse itself.

Tokyo Saiban

Kabe Atsuki Heya—The Thick-Walled Room, also translatable as *Room with thick walls*—marks Kobayashi's first in a series of indictments against war, and the faulted record of human history, which will include the epic, six-part, *Ningen no jōken* (*The Human Condition*, 1959-1961, based on a bestselling novel by Gomikawa Junpei), and the exquisitely restrained *Seppuku* (released in English as *Hara-kiri*, 1962). The stone reliefs that introduce each of the episodes of *Ningen no jōken*, suggestive of Han Dynasty tomb-chamber doors, with contemporary depictions of increasingly disconsolate scenes of modern warfare, offer entry into the world as entombment, with its stamped hollow bricks framing garden gates that are only able to open in, and covering surfaces left uninscribed in the opening shots of *Kabe atsuki heya*. "Stones," writes Frédérique Guétat-Liviani in *espèce*, "have knowledge of settlement."[6]

The film was completed shortly after the nominal end of the U.S. occupation of Japan, not long after the Tokyo Trial's 27-month tenure, and during the entirety of which, indeed extending from 1945 into 1952, Japan was prohibited from any and all critical discussion of the atomic bombs, a tyrannical injunction with which the press complied. Less effective than its counterpart in Germany, the Nuremberg Trial, the Tokyo Trial, with its marked inequalities, was

---

6. "Les pierres connaissent l'échéance." Frédérique Guétat-Liviani. *espèce*. Le temps des cerises. Ivry, 2017 (48). The poem from which this line is pulled, as well as several others, are published in an English translation in *TriQuarterly Magazine*, issue 153, Winter/Spring 2018.

carried out in a theatre of equally careful execution of design. According to journalist Mark Gayn, in his *Japan Diary* (1948), not only was the courtroom, during its construction, "ripped up because it was felt that it did not live up to the importance of the occasion,"[7] at its first session "all that was shown was a very large and photogenic room. Its relative unimportance was betrayed by the first act of inanity."[8] Gayn was referring to a moment when, in the dock, ultra-nationalist philosopher and spy, Okawa Shumei, who was later found to be suffering from tertiary syphillis, suddenly "leaned forward and hit [wartime prime minister] Tōjō Hideki on the head with a rolled copy of the indictment."

By the time the four-and-a-half-hour *Tokyo Saiban—Tokyo Trial*—is being prepared, Sugamo Prison, which is at the centre of the moment in history it addresses, has already been demolished, including the prisoners' vegetable garden. Designed by U.S.-trained architect Yorinaka Tsumaki after several years of further study in Germany, it was officially opened in 1895. Constructed over a four-year period, the 'international' prison, destined to hold prisoners from the west, had a 1.6 km perimeter, which was encircled by a brick wall 5 metres high. Its main gate, 4 metres tall, was made of wood reinforced with iron. Inside the compound, two small watchtowers each presided over five large cell blocks designed to hold two thousand four hundred prisoners, with several housed to a cell.[9] It was destroyed in 1971, having been spared in the carpet bombing of Tokyo, and in its place, what was then Japan's tallest residential shopping complex was erected.

7. *Japan Diary.* William Sloane Associates. New York, 1948 (201).
8. *Ibid.* (209).
9. For further details see Daniel V. Botsman. *Punishment and Power in the Making of Modern Japan.* Princeton University Press. Princeton (NJ), 2005.

The memory of the prison's monumentality, of its architecture, is imbued with "the precarious experience of its very fragility."[10]

There are no secrets left to be revealed in the over-exposures of the real. Such that there are *only ever secrets* rendered invisible in the saturated field, now that everything claims to have been over-seen. If the French verb *traduire* denotes the transference of a person from one place to another, most notably a prisoner, an expressly juridical sense is given to the expression *traduire en justice*—literally *to translate into justice*—and which refers idiomatically to a convocation before a judge or tribunal. This emphasis further inflects the already fraught interchanges by which translation inculpates itself, for the very reason that the *remains* produced by translation and which it thereby oversees, now reified, now displaced, sit under its intractable judgment. The mis-qualified *prison-house of language*[11] reveals and records, to its historical advantage what Ingeborg Bachmann writes as "this trembling restlessness in the night."[12]

If the prison house—like the cage that incarcerates animals—*la jaula*—in which Pizarnik's "I" vests herself in cinders—remains intractable in its construction, with its persuasive methods of

10. Jacques Derrida. *Force de loi*. Galilée. Paris, 1994-2005 (105).

11. Given currency by Friedric Jameson whose use of this expression seems to have been derived from an essay by Eric Heller, "Nietzsche and Wittgenstein," in which "Heller provides a quite loose and poetic translation of Nietzsche's actual words from *Die Wille Zur Macht*, [...] making a metaphor [prison-house] out of *Zwange*, constraint." See David Lovekin. *Technique, Discourse, and Consciousness: An Introduction to the Philosophy of Jacques Ellul*. Associated University Presses. Cranbury (NJ), 1991 (209).

12. Ingeborg Bachmann. *Three Paths to the Lake*, tr. Mary Fran Gilbert. Holmes & Meier. New York, 1989.

enclosure, exclusion, and extinction by means of execution, it relies on capital methods of encapsulation. And it is by means of these methods, that something of the *real* traverses the imposing limits with their gaping shadows, wounded light that succeeds eventually in loosening the structure from its certitudes, and introduces temporal and often untimely indistinctions that prove to be as fatal as the "horrible hammer blows"[13] delivered to stone. In any case they present themselves as more convincing in their arguments than the stark outlines of confinement to which they are subjected. This is as true for Lieutenant Hamada, whose criminal liberty is assured by his obsequious manipulations, as it is for the incarcerated soldier Kawanishi for whom the walls become projectiles against which he can only throw himself, until he commits himself to an extra-judicial hanging, donning "the gardener's gloves" of the hangman.[14] Here is where the prison structure reveals some of its insidious duplicitousness, folding and enfolding its own magnitude into its most intimate interstices—"where time accumulates heavily".[15]

No one is in some garden: what I have named here are solitudes. Solitudes each with their evacuated possessive, and encirlced by fields in which *algo ha muerto, la noche*—something has died, the night. Some thing, for which there is *no one: ningun está en algún jardín.*

---

13. Oscar Wilde. "The Ballad of Reading Gaol" (1896), in *Plays, Prose Writings, and Poems*. Everyman's Library. New York, 1930. (661: "He does not rise in piteous haste / To put on convict-clothes, / While some coarse-mouthed Doctor gloats, and notes / Each new and nerve-twitched pose, / Fingering a watch whose little ticks / Are like horrible hammer-blows.")

14. *Ibid*. ("He does now know that sickening thirst / That sands one's throat, before / The hangman with his gardener's gloves / Slips through the padded door, / And binds one with three leathern thongs, / That the throat may thirst no more.")

15. Takami Jun, "Fingernails of the Dead," in *Anthology of Modern Japanese Poetry*, tr. Edith Marcombe Shiffert and Yūki Sawa. Tuttle. Rutland (VT), 1972 (108).

In the deepest fathoms of the earth's seas are creatures which in French are referred to as *abyssal fish*: they implode when removed from their depths.[16] Before them, and in their intimated absence, one may well ask, with Pizarnik, and with utter knowledge of the murderous charge of one's question: *¿Sos real?*——Are you real?

(November 2017)[17]

---

16. *Le poisson abyssal* entered the space of my thinking in correspondence with Olivia Tapiero, to whom I am grateful, for this, and other sensibilities.

17. The following postface to the text may or may not have been read to the group assembled, but its question was posed despite the persistent enquiry, from several present, as to the relevance of such deliberations among "artists": I'll end here, because here begins our conversation. It is one that is already engaging with the texts Matthew [Girson] suggested that we read today. Celan's *The Meridian*, with its dialogical emphasis, its positioning before a you that is evocative of Martin Buber, but that also invokes the work of Osip Mandelstamm (whom Celan had himself translated), and of course, more evidently, that of Georg Büchner (though it is of interest to note that in Myriam Suchet's reading of Celan's speech, she finds very little variation between it and a text he read on the radio, specifically addressing Mandelstamm's work). And similarly, when Blanchot's own text, taken from *L'espace littéraire*, invokes Orpheus, it is the Orpheus of Rilke's sonnets to whom is owed this particular night, and its other. It is also, I think, not incidental, to note, that during the pre-war years and into the middle of the war, Blanchot's writings were divided into daytime or journalistic writings, and night writings. If the night was given to literary endeavours, the day was given to provocative contributions to the papers of the Catholic far-right in France, in which circles, notwithstanding his lifelong friendship with Emmanuel Lévinas, he was known as an agitator, some would say a fascist, in any case a nationalist. Blanchot's long (journalistic) silence after the war remains as vexed as Heidegger's, with the marked difference of Blanchot's engagement for the duration of his life as a writer, with WWII, and more specifically the Sho'ah.

Pizarnik, for me, touches upon all of these spaces, of night and of appeal, and of intractable violence.

But before naming those aspects further, before sounding these various nights, I propose that we begin in solitude, which is where Blanchot begins

Selective Bibliography — "We give our lives for nothing" and "The Open, Under Cover"

Ingeborg Bachmann. *Three Paths to the Lake*, tr. Mary Fran Gilbert. Holmes and Meier. New York, 1989.

Walter Benjamin. "Critique of Violence" in *Reflections*, tr. Edmund Jephcott. Schocken. New York, 1978 [1921].

Claude R. Blouin. *Le chemin détourné: essai sur Kobayashi et le cinéma japonais.* Hurtubise. Lasalle (QC), 1982.

Claude R. Blouin. "La route de Masaki Kobayashi," in *Shomingeki.*

Daniel V. Botsman. *Punishment and Power in the Making of Modern Japan.* Princeton University Press. Princeton (NJ), 2005.

Penelope Curtis and Caroline Vout. *Antinous: the face of the Antique.* Henry Moore Institute. Leeds, 2006.

Jacques Derrida. *Force de loi.* Galilée. Paris, 1994-2005.

Edward J. Drea. *Researching Japanese War Crimes.* Nazi War Crimes and Japanese Imperial Government Records Interagency Working Group. Washington (DC), 2006.

Futamura Madoka. "Japanese Societal Attitudes Towards the Tokyo Trial: A Contemporary Perspective," in *The Asia-Pacific Journal*, vol. 9, issue 29, no. 5 (July 19, 2011).

Mark Gayn. *Japan Diary.* William Sloane Ass. New York, 1948.

John L. Ginn. *Sugamo Prison, Tokyo: An Account of the Trial and Sentencing of Japanese War Criminals in 1948, by a U.S. Participant.* McFarland & Co. Jefferson [NC], 1992.

Andrea Grunert. "Masaki Kobayashi," in *Sense of Cinema*, issue 79 (July 2016).

Linda Hoagland. "A Conversation with Kobayashi Masaki," in *Positions: East Asia Cultures Critique*, vol. 2, issue 2 (1994; 384-402).

Franz Kafka. *Journal intime*, tr. Pierre Klossowski. Payot & Rivages. Paris, 2008.

Donald Keene. *So Lovely a Country Will Never Perish.* Columbia University Press. New York, 2010.

Krzysztof Loska. "Kobayashi Masaki and the Legacy of the World War II," in *Silva Iaponicarum*, issue 43-46 (68-81).

Joan Mellen. *Voices from the Japanese Cinema.* Liveright. New York, 1975.

Ōoka Shōhei. *Journal d'un prisonnier de guerre*, tr. François Compoint. Belin. Paris, 2006 [1952].

---

in *L'espace littéraire*, a literary and artistic solitude. And so Matthew, before arriving at the other night, I wish to ask you: *what of solitude* which is present in both of the texts you invited us to read toward this afternoon?

Sōseki Natsume. *À travers la vitre*, tr. René de Ceccatty and Ryōji Nakamura. Payot & Rivages. Paris, 1993.

Pier Paolo Pasolini. *L'expérience hérétique*, tr. Anna Rocchi Pullberg. Payot. Paris, 1976.

Pier Paolo Pasolini. *Heretical Empiricism*, tr. Ben Lawton and Louise K. Barnett. New Academia Publishing. Washington (DC), 2005 [1998].

Lindsey Powell and Chunmei Du. "Escaping Sugamo Prison with a no. 2 pencil: the drawings of Japanese war criminal Tobita Tokio," in *Visual Studies*, vol. 30, no. 1 (2015; 1-18).

Yūki Sawa. *Anthology of Modern Japanese Poetry*, tr. Edith Marcombe and Yūki Sawa. Charles E. Tuttle. Tokyo, 1972.

William Shakespeare. *Complete Works*. Oxford University Press. London, 1965 [1905; 1603].

Françoise Wera. "Entretien avec Masaki Kobayashi," vol. 5, no. 2 (November 1985/January 1986; 22-24).

Alula,   for posterity
(Autobiography of Translation)

Is what is named not already lost?

ALBERT CAMUS

He had two rooms on the same floor.

INGEBORG BACHMANN

If a translator stands both before and after, it is in part out of desperation. And so why not, in such an instance, (I mean in an instance in which one is called upon to speak of something when one has no inclination to do so—) state things clearly, if one is to have any chance at all—knowing that chance is full of misgivings, and that wagering on it may result in deceitful strategies that may lead one, full of bravura, to declare, and for the record: "I make my own luck." Setting off a series of dictatorships that move back and forth between the drawing room and the gambling table, the city street and the air strip, incriminating the cinema with its highest (most base) aspirations. It is good to remember that Delphine Seyrig, in *L'année dernière à Marienbad*, is a broken-necked bird, and the revolver signifies an intention. The phantasm of the stalker is tired and remote, and yet stands at every yawning door, with its perfidious eventuality scripted into the most high-minded of aspirations, in which the most disposable bodies are made to keep silent while inwardly they scream. But do not misunderstand me: the scream emerges eventually, as it did, with persistence, from Michael Lonsdale's throat, and by his own admission, he was in fact, the Vice-Consul, *in love*, with Delphine Seyrig or Anne-Marie Stretter, firing blindly into the sweltering colonial night. (The fish, too, screams, with Ingeborg Bachmann: ": here, I can feel it right here."—", he had

wanted to shoot it [the cernia] in the back of the neck."[1]
And the camel (*Franza*), and so on.)

"Who shouted out of me?"[2]

A translator is equally capable of screaming, but it is not for
the usual reasons of hidden names and relegation. At times
one *wishes* to be relegated and to avert prominence without
abandoning one's responsibilities: I mean to *meet a person
there*. To travel that distance along a shrieking rail line
beneath an overwrought sun, with one's eyes full of sweat
and cramps in one's stomach, only to sit and listen with both
ears and the full extent of the organ of one's perforated skin,
to enter the vibrations of a low-speaking voice, and to know
that whatever one's efforts, the words will seep through the
available membranes adopting various forms of distortion
that cannot be carried back with one's hands and nor can
they be confided to another. One might well aspire, with
René Char, to be "intelligent and mute, contained and
revolted,"[3] but the *muteness* in question is one that cannot
be explained or gratified with recognition. The necessary
motions (it seems to me) are *down* and *in* and not *up* and *out*.

And if this recourse to antonyms seems overly simplistic
for this age of obfuscation, I refer you to an early essay
(1935-1936) by Albert Camus, which appears in *L'Envers et
l'endroit*, specifically the one titled "Entre oui et non". This
one because it may be, that, having only read *L'homme révolté*

---

1. Ingeborg Bachmann. *Three Paths to the Lake*, tr. Mary Fran Gilbert.
Holmes & Meier. New York, 1989 (32).

2. Ingeborg Bachmann. *The Thirtieth Year*, tr. M. Bullock. Holmes &
Meier. New York, 1987 (170).

3. René Char. *Recherche de la base et du sommet*. Gallimard. Paris, 1971
[1955] (9).

in English, and with the various accommodations made to the text, the extremities of this language may have escaped your reading ear by virtue of their *attenuation*. (The painter loved the word *attenuate*, he used it at every turn, by which I mean *often*, and ever more often to mean its opposite, *augment*, which he pronounced *aug-u-ment*, which was both charming and confounding, since something sinister had seemed to enter the word there, in the manner, perhaps, of an *unguent*, something oily and not quite pleasing to the ear, presented as a salve, but potentially full of poison—a sort of sea urchin in language, which, when admired at a distance is much preferable to its needles projected into one's skin, though it would never occur to one to *kill it*). On the matter of "oui" and "non," which is given short shrift in *The Rebel*,[4] where it appears under the guise of "the affirmative" and "the negative," one senses an immediate form of apology, extended well beyond the sorts of niceties to which a translator may be inclined to conform. Which is of course obedience to a form of tyranny, the origins of which remain unclear but are certainly traceable to the apprenticeship of every manner of hypocrisy (and compromise) on which social contracts are written, into and including those that lead quite virtuously to murder (not incidentally a question that preoccupied the author of these works until his death, and cost him, of course, the friendship of his greedy little peers, who preferred, as do most *private hunting grounds* the privilege of the kill). Camus writes, at the close of "Entre oui et non:" "Don't let them say about the man condemned to death: 'He is going to pay his debt to society,' but 'They're going to chop his head off.'"[5]

4. Albert Camus, *The Rebel: An Essay on Man in Revolt*, tr. Anthony Bower. Alfred A. Knopf. New York, 1954.

5. Albert Camus, *Lyrical and Critical Essays*, tr. Ellen Conroy Kennedy. Vintage Books. New York, 1970 [1967] (39).

Translation is a name by which a work falls into competition with itself.

I had not wanted to speak of any of this. It is not that the *I* is hidden, but it is entitled to its reluctance. A reluctance to invoke an incontinent memory abandoned to a present whose calculated imperviousness is a menial form of survival. For the sake of its own oblivion, it doesn't repeat itself. And what this makes of time is just as pernicious as the various itineraries mapped onto it. I suppose one could write an autobiography of translation that would have, of necessity, to account for the blank overlays. I don't see how it could be done otherwise, and with so many cans of film sitting at the inflamed bottoms of the oceans. Could you hold your breath that far I wonder? Any given indication would be misleading. Because translation in itself is a *breach of conduct.* (In 2003, I fell asleep in Frankfurt, between Montréal and Ljubljana; the assigned waiting area matched the number on my boarding pass, but it was another traveller who, having seen me alight from the same flight, woke me in the midst of the empty room because the gate number had been changed at the last minute. This is exactly what I am talking about). Good intentions, etc. One such itinerary might extend from Dany Bébel-Gisler (*Léonora*) all the way to Kafū Nagai, with a brief excursion to the northern edge of the African continent, I mean by boat, of course, among the astragalus and the gabians (genus: *larus*) of the limestone islands, I mean out of reach of the continent, I mean a stone's throw from Oran, which, in Berber, is a lion (an ontological emphasis is immediately installed in the sentence), which redirects me implacably to Lyon, and so on. Geography provides an utterly unreliable transcript of one's displacements, preferring the haphazard vectors of emotion, which enable one to imagine a place to be beautiful (the light in Antibes, or the crowded medinas of Marseille) when in fact the bathroom ceiling is leaking brown water into the shower, and at the bottom of the hill in the rain, the squid is already being strangled: it is too late. The bulls, too, are screaming, in the empty arenas of Arles where the *feria* is eternal and eternally condemnable until such time as the human is rendered extinct.

Of course the river (Sumida) is as important as the purchase of a hat. Bearing in mind that in the course of waiting (expectation), *nothing really happens.*

—

Out of the name that by its own admission is intolerable, it becomes evident that even an annihilated body prefers its suppression to the reduction of its movements. So it relegates itself to a mistaken itinerary, it chooses destitution, it says *I* to the point of depletion without evoking an anterior state, a fixed address, the dislocation of its articulations undermined by one or several forms of hesitation, a hastened acceptation of a disavowed watchword. In the Château Rothschild at Boulogne-Billancourt, there had been Göring (1942) and then the cameras (1976) at a thirty-year interval, and whereas the ceiling was falling in, the film was shot in the dark, the window, pierced by a bullet, allowed for the infiltration of what was assuredly atomic light, and the cracked stones registered the footsteps, not those of an undeclared birth year, but those of a desperate architecture, and body drowned at the edge of an inventoried beach assigned to another continent. It had been necessary to travel far, all the way to the finished city in order to accuse the great delay that reigned there, unto the garden of toppled statues, where one's sole means of survival is to steal from oneself.

In the dream that dreams me Kawanishi wakes up screaming. These are the hours preceding the improvised gallows at Sugamo, a now-demolished Tokyo prison that bore the name of a fibrous waterweed out of which paper can be wrought, or an ersatz of cotton, strong enough for hanging B-class war criminals, for whom the walls become projectiles against which they can only throw themselves. In Kobayashi Masaki's filmography, Sugamo Prison stands at either end of his production, between the U.S. occupation of Japan and *Gojira*'s double (1984), duplicated over the course of years, in a persistent investigation into the contemporary crime of war and its insidious adjudication. Through its archival returns, it functions not only as a memory of a recorded place but as the memory of that memory (and by its own postponement, under threat of censorship). A rejection of clemency, despite the judgments handed down at Nuremberg and Tokyo, where the wests were one. (The painter had astonished himself. My admiration came from what he had not done. From the fact that the form, having become its own structure, had refused the "writing" of the bomb.)

An example. On April 18, 1942, the U.S. carried out its first air raid over Japan, during which sixteen medium-range bombers "dropped bombs on what the United States officially described as military targets in Tokyo. [...] The photographs of their accomplishments prove only that they sank a small fishing boat."[6]

---

6. Donald Keene. *So Lovely a Country Will Never Perish*. Columbia University Press. New York, 2010 (21).

Like the legend of the shooting of Liberty Valance,[7] translation relies on methods that are necessarily fictive. The estimated exchange value is perennially posthumous. The present is ever indebted to itself. It is its own archive, and subject to the same kinds of depredations to which are subject the artefacts of war, with particular attention given to the large numbers of missing documents, not to mention the bodies, searched for with equal desperation, as though one were somehow equivalent to the other, with each concealing a hidden script, and in any case, *evidence* of the mutilated forms by which existence must now recuse itself.

Kabe atsuki heya—The Thick-Walled Room, also translatable as *Room with thick walls*—marks Kobayashi's first in a series of indictments against war, and the faulted record of human history, which will include the epic, six-part, *Ningen no jōken* (*The Human Condition*, 1959-1961, based on a bestselling novel by Gomikawa Junpei), and the exquisitely restrained *Seppuku* (released in English as *Hara-kiri*, 1962). The stone reliefs that introduce each of the episodes of *Ningen no jōken*, suggestive of Han Dynasty tomb-chamber doors, with contemporary depictions of increasingly disconsolate scenes of modern warfare, offer entry into the world as entombment, with its stamped hollow bricks framing garden gates that are only able to open in, and covering surfaces left uninscribed in the opening shots of *Kabe atsuki heya*.

---

7. "This is the west, Sir. When the legend becomes fact, print the legend." *The Man Who Shot Liberty Valance* (Directed by John Ford; script by Willis Goldbeck and James Warner Bellah). Ford Productions/Paramount. 1962. This sentence, the sense of which is inverted by Jean-Luc Godard in *Éloge de l'amour* (in English as *In Praise of Love*), shifts *the imprint* toward *obedience*: "quand les faits deviennent / des légendes, il faut / obéir à la légende" (when the facts become / legends, one must / obey the legend). Jean-Luc Godard, *Éloge de l'amour*. P.O.L. Paris, 2001 (89).

"Stones," writes Frédérique Guétat-Liviani in *espèce*, "have knowledge of settlement."[8]

The film was completed shortly after the nominal end of the U.S. occupation of Japan, not long after the Tokyo Trial's 27-month tenure, and during the entirety of which, indeed extending from 1945 into 1952, Japan was prohibited from any and all critical discussion of the atomic bombs, a tyrannical injunction with which the press complied. Less effective than its counterpart in Germany, the Nuremberg Trial, the Tokyo Trial, with its marked inequalities, was carried out in a theatre of equally careful execution of design. According to journalist Mark Gayn, in his *Japan Diary* (1948), not only was the courtroom, during its construction, "ripped up because it was felt that it did not live up to the importance of the occasion,"[9] at its first session "all that was shown was a very large and photogenic room. Its relative unimportance was betrayed by the first act of inanity."[10] Gayn was referring to a moment when, in the dock, ultra-nationalist philosopher and spy, Okawa Shumei, who was later found to be suffering from tertiary syphillis, suddenly "leaned forward and hit [wartime prime minister] Tōjō Hideki on the head with a rolled copy of the indictment."

By the time the four-and-a-half-hour *Tokyo Saiban—Tokyo Trial*—is being prepared, Sugamo Prison, which is at the centre of the moment in history it addresses, has already been demolished, including the brothels that gird the enclave.

---

8. "Les pierres connaissent l'échéance." Frédérique Guétat-Liviani. *espèce*. Le temps des cerises. Ivry, 2017. (48). The poem from which this line is pulled, as well as several others, are published in an English translation in *TriQuarterly Magazine*, issue 153, Winter/Spring 2018.

9. *Japan Diary*. William Sloane Associates. New York, 1948 (201).

10. *Ibid.* (209).

Designed by U.S.-trained architect Yorinaka Tsumaki after several years of study in Germany, it was officially opened in 1895. Constructed over a four-year period, the 'international' prison, destined to hold prisoners from the west, had a 1.6 km perimeter, which was encircled by a brick wall 5 metres high. Its main gate, 4 metres tall, was made of wood reinforced with iron. Inside the compound, two small watchtowers each presided over five large cell blocks designed to hold two thousand four hundred prisoners, with several housed to a cell.[11] It was destroyed in 1971, having been spared in the carpet bombing of Tokyo, and in its place, what was then Japan's tallest residential shopping complex was erected. The memory of the prison's monumentality, of its architecture, is imbued with "the precarious experience of its very fragility."[12]

Who am I to translation in the application for leniency? There are no secrets left to be revealed in the over-exposures of the real. Such that there are *only ever secrets* rendered invisible in the saturated field, now that everything claims to have been over-seen. If the French verb *traduire* denotes the transference of a person from one place to another, most notably a prisoner, an expressly juridical sense is given to the expression *traduire en justice*—literally *to translate into justice*—and which refers idiomatically to a convocation before a judge or tribunal. This emphasis further inflects the already fraught interchanges by which translation inculpates itself, for the very reason that the *remains* produced by translation and which it thereby oversees, now reified, now displaced, sit under its intractable

11. For further details see Daniel V. Botsman. *Punishment and Power in the Making of Modern Japan*. Princeton University Press. Princeton (NJ), 2005.
12. Jacques Derrida. *Force de loi*. Galilée. Paris, 1994-2005 (105).

judgment. The mis-qualified *prison–house of language*[13] reveals and records, to its historical advantage what Bachmann writes as "this trembling restlessness in the night."[14]

There exist four versions of *Son nom de Venise dans Calcutta désert*. In each of these, only one of which is shown, the camera stands in for fear. The torrid nights are filmed in winter, and the cinematographer's hands are frozen at sunset, revivified before a fireplace in the condemned palace, requisitioned first by Nazis who siphoned out the art works, and then the U.S. military, who used the Japanese pagoda for firewood and whose tanks razed the rose garden and the chestnut grove. The grounds, twice since partitioned, once for a hospital, and a second time to accommodate the junction of *autoroute A13* (and by what accident of language does the *autoroute* bear even a nominal relationship to the *autoportrait*, unauthored and reflexively unabashed in its destructiveness, such that neither is able to account for what it pertains to, if only in its way), sits silent still under the guise of its ruin in the umbrage of a single large-leaved linden, some twenty metres tall, in the direction of the long-abolished Japanese garden. If these are not secrets anymore, of the kind kept by *India Song* and ghosted into *Son nom de Venise dans Calcutta*

---

13. Given currency by Friedric Jameson whose use of this expression seems to have been derived from an essay by Eric Heller, "Nietzsche and Wittgenstein," in which "Heller provides a quite loose and poetic translation of Nietzsche's actual words from *Die Wille Zur Macht*, [...] making a metaphor [prison-house] out of *Zwange*, constraint." See David Lovekin. *Technique, Discourse, and Consciousness: An Introduction to the Philosophy of Jacques Ellul.* Associated University Presses. Cranbury (NJ), 1991 (209).

14. Ingeborg Bachmann. *Three Paths to the Lake*, tr. Mary Fran Gilbert. Holmes & Meier. New York, 1989 (11).

désert, where the remaindered voices trace the outlines of figures, each of which grows ever more posthumous with the piano on film, they are the secrets that keep me, in the inadvertent movement between versions.

Why tell such things? This is the way of memory: in the twenty years between myself and a city, only the city remained, with its names and its injuries. It is not me, walking, nor even a phantom, but a form of eradication that bears the cost of this much walking out. When the Austrian philosopher declares that "a man will be *imprisoned* in a room with a door that's unlocked and opens inwards; as long as it does not occur to him to *pull* rather than to push it," he overlooks the problem of indifference, which is this: that a bullet fired at glass will transpierce the body in the way of its shattering.

Perhaps, with Chopin, the question that skirts the edges of posterity is this: *in what way will my corpse be less than me?*[15] When the other one is sleeping, I lose my breath. It is only toward the very end that you see yourself, you, myself, you say, who am watching you fall. It is fleeting and screaming, the gaze carried onto the inability to prevent the fall by which you are consummated, and which falls under the aegis of what I see to the point of seeing preventing the eternalised dream as well as your falling. *Lento ma non troppo*, prelude to nothing.

---

15. Quoted by Jean-Yves Clément in *Les deux âmes de Frédéric Chopin*. Le Passeur. Paris, 2017. Clément quotes from Gronislas Édouard Sydow *et al.*'s translation of Chopin's correspondence, which I have, in turn, rendered into this English.

On the extinction of birds: the few radiographies I have been able to produce reveal the startling existence of a feather deemed (by ornithologists) to be superfluous (I have not gone so far as to determine an equivalency between it, say, and the appendix—appendices have long proved useful if not altogether illuminating for close readers, or, for that matter, again, so-called and very much misattributed wisdom teeth, not to mention adenoids, etc.). My own topographies escape me... But it is possible, that I might adopt the alula as metonym. (*Métonymie*: mental disorder characterised by the incorrect usage of words.)[16] If it is indeed superfluous, unlike the furcula ("wishbone"), instigator of the beating wing, then alula is the name by which *I* falls silent.

(July / October 2017)

---

16. *Littré*, 1880.

The letter is a letter of refusal addressed to no one.

Addendum
—

Of the two gardens,

It is much later that I arrive at you.

By which I mean on the other side of the written letter.

It is by the letter that I find myself summoned, it is far from it that I follow you.

In the state in which I find myself, before you, in this place of lake and of garden, of fragile geography.

Its distance is henceforth extinguished.

It is extinguished, at all times, in the present, on the verge of the body which lives in me, against me, and the sea, its landswell.

In the crush of times, surging and abated.

In the interstice of rendering, its parcel, its congealment, turned, hunted from there.

Of the two gardens, I will not choose one. Not the one in which the path is displaced under the feet of the dead having fallen there, the heron and the goose, and the human child whose calcareous name is burned by the sun of Oran, by the street of beating doors, and the ferry that seeks to flee the continent.

Nor that of Shalimar where the cries dissolve in the shots of the gun drawn in the colonial night against the bodies eaten by the monsoon and waiting, a heat, of its own.

It is said that "nothing resembles a prison more than another prison."[1]

Five hundred blows delivered before the disappearing doorways, and whose names dissolve against the walls of the executed, and the other, who says *I* before you, in absentia.

Nadie está en algún jardín.[2]

—

The letter is a letter of refusal, addressed to no one.

The garden is a capsized ship, a cemetery of cetacea, and the ship, all of interiors,[3] turns its face progressively away from its evacuated gaze.

—

1. Étienne Jaudel. *Le Procès de Tokyo*. Odile Jacob. Paris, 2010 (7).
2. Alejandra Pizarnik.
3. "L'événement devient intérieur au navire." Léon Werth, *Cochinchine*. Viviane Hamy. P7aris, 1997 [1926] (15). (The event becomes internal to the ship).

Arrêt sur visage

or else isolated in silence

Danielle Collobert

In the language of film there are often extraordinary divergences between English and French, which prove at times to be irreconcilable.[1]

If this tendency toward discrepancy is true of translation *as a rule*, it reveals itself to be *particularly* true in the case of this work in translation.

Danielle Collobert's *Recherche*,[2] rendered as *Research*, in which the *search* of re-search, must be read as detachable, with emphasis on its repetitive motion—but also in its slide from substantive to predicate (search>searches)—, makes salient such divergences, through the implied camera movement panning over the evacuated faces of A and B and the marked distances especially that define the space of their bodies, in proximity and in remove, as though the text were annotating a form of recusal that is implicit in the spaces of desire to which their mortiferous movements owe everything; an intimacy of anticipated death, and seizure, from which the camera extracts movements of degradation through violent stillness.

---

1. The term *découpage* offers an immediate case in point, and one which has been the source of much confusion. See, in this respect, Timothy Barnard's *découpage*. Caboose. Montréal, 2014.

2. Published in English in the volume, *In the Environs of a Film* by Danielle Collobert, tr. Nathanaël. Litmus Press. New York, 2019.

Indeed the term *still* here is adopted to render the French *arrêt*, proposing a false equivalency between the (film) still and its seemingly concordant locution, the arrêt (sur image). These are "attested" terms and which reveal something of the contexts in which each seeks to function. In *Recherche* Collobert limits herself to the use of *arrêt sur* designating in each instance a specific detail on which the camera is to *stop*. "Stop" of course is one of the translations of the lone substantive "arrêt," which also implies "arrest," (from the verb *arrêter*) replete with its juridical (enforceable/enforcible) intent.[3]

One might just as readily translate "arrêt sur" as "stop at," stopping at nothing to achieve the irresistible demands of such a transitive language that subverts its own objectivity through a persistent preference for passive forms, abdicating responsibility to the law in abject deference to its capital aims. Regimens of grammar are coincident with regimens of power now as always.[4]

More than one frontier has now been crossed, and reading the three works[5] gathered by Françoise Morvan under the title *Expériences* (experiments and/or experiences) in this so-called America is a serious transposition indeed in which

3. As in Maurice Blanchot's *Arrêt de mort*—death sentence—written in that uncomfortable interstice between Blanchot's writings as a fascist agitator in Vichy France and his literary refashioning of himself on the far-left, in the silence for which he was known, and which may be read as a sentence reiteratively pronounced against himself, in secret. A sentence which carries the secret of its arrest, a non-permutable secret, in other words irrevocable following French law, a sentence to be served in full, that is, unto death, its imminent postponement.

4. Indeed, the multiplication of *regards*—gazes, looks, stares—in both *Recherche* and *Polyphonie* evokes the *eye of the law*, which, in the seemingly lawless contexts of the work, is no less forceful in its application of surveillance.

5. *Recherche, Polyphonie, Ça des mots.*

the sands of north-western France adjoining the virulent Atlantic, may readily allow themselves to be supplanted by an imagined *far-ouest* of burnt deserts shimmering with radioactive particulate, under some gun. These are voided investigations that succeed only in subtracting the body from its criminality—a condemnation of ages pressed into moments, a crime committed to each and every one.

Meurtre (*Murder*), the title of Collobert's first acknowledged work[6] is just as operative in these cinematic and radiophonic works; indeed it can be read as a *mot d'ordre* for her entire oeuvre,[7] and with which its entire topography is suffused. The *stills* of "Recherche" and "Polyphonie" attest to this, as does the recurrence of the isolate *arrêt* whether in its designation of a bus stop or a pause in action (breaks in the fight, for example, between B and the man on the dock), toppling into the near untranslatable *arrêts* in the plural, *stops*, which invites, again, a transitive reading rather than the congealment of the plural substantive, and this, in keeping with the stares that transfix and bore into the faces verging on the dunes. The polysemic displacement of *arrêt* is such that the cumulative effect of its multiply transposed sense is that of a film strip caught in a projector, and it isn't clear whether the image is held or whether it is caught in the mechanism; in either case the reader is among those held captive by a language that forbids

---

6. Collobert not only disavowed but destroyed her first published book, *Chants des guerres* (*Songs of* [*the*] *wars*, 1961) within several years of its first printing.

7. As is the case for the oeuvre of Ingeborg Bachmann whose *Todesarten* (in English as "ways of dying") cycle of works is similarly underwritten by the extension of war into unacknowledged spaces of intimacy: "Indeed, I maintain and will only attempt to produce the first evidence that still today many people do not die but are murdered." (From the "Foreword" to *Das Buch Franza* [*The Book of Franza*], tr. Peter Filkins. Northwestern University Press. Evanston (IL), 1999, [4]).

release, burrowing instead, more deeply, into a thickeningly menacing interiority with its inscription of fear similar to that elicited by the perceived approach of the *beast* in Kafka's "Burrow." The time of exposure holds the permanent promise of such a threat.

(March 2018)

Effacements -- turns, to torn suns

*The blindness I refer to here need not mean only
the blindness of the eyes.*

KAWABATA YASUNARI

When Albert Camus writes, in praise of René Char, that "the woman lost her face," he is already drawing an outline of an autobiography that will never be able to be written, interrupted at the outset by disappearance. And yet, all reflexivity *depends* upon disappearance, whence not only its necessity, but its fugitive occurrence. For even its fleeting is only answerable for what is said to be *past*, a face, in the absence of the name attributed to it, or again the name detached from its drowning. The *I* from which everything proceeds and according to which the lure of (af)filiation is closed speaks precisely of this loophole. And the face that persists in rising to the surfaces of liquidated memories is the sole promise of anonymity which intimates being and non-being. An imprint of the damaged centuries, rubbed on the walls of caverns exposed to desert winds, turned toward a torn sun, turned away, at last, from its burn. So that those of us who see it are able to say of it, at last, that it is lost, the face, as well as its recognition.

It may be that the cinema, more than any other art form, exposes the posthumous condition of its viewer. Perhaps it is in this that it recuses so forcefully its debt to literature. If, as Marguerite Duras insists, the cinema is built upon the defeat of writing—indeed, its massacre—it is writing's latency that makes the cinema impossible. It writes itself as a letter and like a letter it burns, at the surfaces of the many seas that announce its capsize.

Like the photograph, its twin, inscribed in light, it burns out, the sky and its night.

If it is its own memory, it is forgotten to history, as only memory can be:

> pages fallen from a ripped screen, avid for the dry riverbed, starved of its migration, given to abandon—

It is this face, exactly, which we are given to see, and whose disfigurement may be the twin result of a desire to be seen and the damage done by looking. Such that there is no further semblance possible, and the dream that murders the dream, is cast in time with the same prison whose walls enclose a garden for the living.

(June 2018)

The time of exposure is never

Antinoüs: Hadrian's young suicided lover, half of whose face sits in Rome, at the Palazzo Altemps, and the other half in Chicago, at the Art Institute.[1] Figure of an afflicted Europe and an America forever done over, on the one hand his face is falsely reconstituted, on the other left in a state of ruin, gaping and fractured, and from this doubling surfaces a vexation, a thought torn apart on the shores of two drowned continents. The lover, so split, suddenly finds himself subject to an enchainment of echoes, each revealing itself to be more distanced than the other, from podium to podium, and from imitation to imitation, and from which he is irremediably torn, implanted, overthrown, and supplanted. Even identified, the face no longer belongs to itself, as it is deported toward zones of post-mortal auscultation following a method reserved for exhumed corpses.[2]

Antinoüs, forerunner of ancient desires, whose livid body is fished repeatedly from the waters of an immortally stylised Nile, a water

---

1. Sombre edifice flanked at its front doors by two bronze verdigris lions, who, in another age would have drowned there, since the lake, until 1855, reached as far as what is now Michigan Avenue. The museum, like everything that extends east from its edifice all the way to the (false) limit of the water (sometimes at a kilometre's distance), is set upon in-fill—including the remains of the burned city of 1871.
2. See, in this respect, *Megeles's Skull*. Sternberg Press/Portikus. Berlin/Frankfurt-Am-Main, 2012.

envied for having wrapped into its intimacy the body of the lover
abandoned to the surf, is he not, himself, Antinoüs, held at a distance,
each time he is named, and renowned, by the foremen of ancient
history, who by way of his face introduce themselves into his body
with the sole objective of citing, if not situating him, while pushing
aside Hadrian, spectator : in other words by adopting the point of
view of empire. It is a rending tribunal which, by the proliferated
replica of the face under different countenances, undertakes a
sustained examination the flagrant indiscretion of which commits
to the adjudication of his identity, in which the unique Antinoüs
disappears under the mise-en-abyme of infinitely scrutinised traits
by which he is adored, in his name alone, extracted from the place
of his disappearance, under the dumbfounded gaze of history.

The body of flesh at the moment at which it touches the mortiferous
water emerges of stone, petrified by its disappearance which will be
legendary, and which will confer him his singularity.

—

Nantes : 1943. "More decisively" yet than the bombings that
modified it, the city experienced "a mutation of a rarer kind.
The in-fill of the arms of the Loire between the islands, the
in-fill of the Erdre at the centre of Nantes, changed forever
its equilibrium and its basis, whereas the rail line was buried,
staked by its three successive train stations, which traversed
the heart of the city between the barriers of the level crossings,
just like a mining settlement of the Far-West."[3] The draining
of the arms of the Loire moreover revealed the remains of a
massacre dating back to the Revolution, which this "fluvial
cemetery" concealed.[4]

---

3. Julien Gracq. *La forme d'une ville.* José Corti. Paris, 1985 (8).
4. "The eleven drownings in the Loire, which made five thousand victims,

Out of these unforgotten strata emerges a stain ; a film fogs over and catches fire. Dispossessed of its forms, it makes one as it wishes, and its echo justifies its disappearance. "As for the *truth*, will I admit to you? it is of no concern to me at all. I do not seek it—I flee it. And I consider that to be my *true* duty."[5] The city thus deported places its seal upon the forbidden letter which never will be written. The body runs, as does the place. It is the assignation of the untranslatable, and its missed act, translation.[6] To translate the untranslatable is to renounce the occidentality of transparency, and to devote oneself to the opaque traversal of invisible limits—an "arduous opacity"[7] whose apocalypse[8] is dependent precisely upon the buckling of

---

exceed in horror the massacres of Parisian prisons. The refractory priests, who had been directed to Nantes to be deported, were piled onto pontoons and barges pierced with holes just above the floatation line in order to scuttle them." Louis Réau. *Histoire du vandalisme. Les monuments détruits de l'art français*, tome I. Hachette. Paris, 1959 (204).

5. Claude Cahun. *Héroïnes*. Mille et une nuits. Paris, 2006 (100). Héroïnes—the book—is a posthumous invention. The writing of these texts coincides with the writing of *Aveux non avenus*; a third of them were not published during the author's lifetime.

6. ": translation is the a priori of the untranslatable." Naoki Sakai. *Translation & Subjectivity: On 'Japan' and Cultural Nationalism*. University of Minnesota Press. Minneapolis (MN), 1997 (5).

7. L'éclair du cri, l'opacité ardue de la parole. (The flash of the cry, the arduous opacity of speech.) Édouard Glissant. *L'intention poétique*. Seuil. Paris, 1969 (194).

8. "*Apokaluptô*, je découvre, je dévoile, je révèle la chose qui peut être une partie du corps, la tête ou les yeux, une partie secrète, le sexe ou quoi que ce soit de caché, un secret, une chose qui ne se montre ni ne se dit, se signifie peut-être mais ne peut ou ne doit pas être livrée d'abord à l'évidence." (Apokaluptô, *I dis-cover, I unveil, I reveal the thing that can be a part of the body, the head or the eyes, a secret part, the sex or whatever might be hidden, a secret, a thing that is neither shown nor said, signified perhaps but that cannot or must not first be delivered up to self-evidence.*) Jacques Derrida. *D'un ton apocalyptique adopté naguère en philosophie*. Galilée. Paris, 1983 (11-12). In English as *Of an Apocalyptic Tone Recently Adopted in Philosophy*, tr. John P.

knowledge before its own arrogance. If the fettering of truth conditions such an assumption, the "true" to which Claude Cahun lays claim will be its unverifiable exutory, ceaselessly diverted by its own conditions. Is there a city that can claim otherwise?

—

The (human) body is a thought that writes itself into the recusal of oblivion. It poses itself as a question, eminently secret, it is given, by its flight, to the public square. And that from which it liberates itself is inscribed in the folds of its *actualism*.[9] If migrations destroy the idea one can have of a geography, it is that the time that binds them is indestructible. In this its "accident is essential and fatal."[10] And the name which is attributed to it, even when spoken, ineluctably escapes nomination. A history without markers, and yet with numerous anchorages, with islands adrift off the coast of some continent, it is populated with oil-slicked birds, oil spills, weathered waves, and gouged gazes.

The twentieth century speaks volumes as to the expectations the author Claude Cahun will have imposed upon her age. If she was born before her name, it was, one might imagine

---

Leavy Jr., in *Oxford Literary Review*, vol. 6, no. 2, 1984 (4).

9. "Doctrine selon laquelle les phénomènes géologiques du passé s'expliquent de la même manière que les phénomènes actuellement observables, ce qui exclut les catastrophes planétaires imaginées pour rendre compte des grands événements tectoniques et des successions de faunes et de flores." (*Doctrine according to which the geological phenomena of the past are explained in the same way as currently observable phenomena, which excludes planetary catastrophes imagined to account for the great tectonic events and successions of fauna and flora.*) Dictionnaire Larousse.

10. Jacques Derrida. *Demeure, Athènes*. Galilée. Paris, 2009 (12).

(but imagine only) in order to gather into her body scarcely arrived at its vitality the tides of an ending century which will have accomplished, on the one hand the (nominal) abolition of slaveries, for which the city of her birth will have been one of the principal centres of the Atlantic trade;[11] and on the other hand will have been the miscreant witness both of the Dreyfus Affair,[12] and the trials of Oscar Wilde, the tragic consequences of which are amply known. If Claude Cahun is a name among others which the author will have adopted as a signature for her writings, it is the one that fully escapes pseudonymy; the author will have *embodied* it.[13] A body carrying the responsibility of a truth that escapes the assigned language, and flies into the air on clipped wings. "I console myself (poorly) in thinking that I seized my only chance of being missed...... "[14]

---

11. "Incontestable capital of the French trade throughout the 18th century, [Nantes] vigorously reasserts itself at the head of the traffic after 1815, and persists, whereas others progressively abandon this traffic. In total, for close to a century and a half, the trade will thus have accompanied the history of Nantes." In effect, "[Nantes's share] in the French trade experiences highs [after 1825, whereas the other French ports have abandoned the trade] reaching close to 70% after the restoration." The role played by Nantes in the Atlantic trade exceeds even the status of Liverpool, "the world capital of the Atlantic trade during the 18th century, [...] even though the latter alone launches as many slave ships as all of France. Trade does in effect play a role much inferior to the one it fulfils in Nantes." Olivier Pétré-Grenouilleau. *Nantes au temps de la traite des Noirs*. Hachette. Paris, 1998 (225 and 7).

12. ...the anti-semitic outcome of which will provoke the expedition of Cahun, as a child, to Surrey, in the south-east of England, and toward the English language she will practise in her texts.

13. She herself affirms in a letter to Charles-Henri Barbier dated January 21, 1951: "Claude Cahun [...] représentait (représente à mes yeux) mon véritable nom plutôt qu'un pseudonyme." (*Claude Cahun [...] represented (represents in my eyes) my veritable name rather than a pseudonym.*) Quoted by François Lerperlier in *Écrits*, op. cit. (41).

14. Claude Cahun. *Aveux non avenus* [1930], in *Écrits, op. cit.* (86).

In 1967, off the coasts of Armor, the Liberian tanker *Torrey Canyon* capsized between the Isles of Scilly and the British coast, dumping 121,000 tons of crude oil into the English Channel. It is estimated that 15,000 seabirds were exterminated. As for the oil slick, it only skimmed the edges of the Isle of Jersey. Not far from there, an oil-slicked Puffin emerging from the "brown surf" beat its "sticky wings." In its congealed wings, *history* was caught;[15] and no gaze in its face,[16] as is able to testify the Colonel Philippe Milon, conservationist at Sept-Îles sanctuary at Perros-Guirec: "in the place of the moist globe that played without blinking in the sea, there were two holes full of fuel..."[17]

Here ends the *L'Histoire naturelle des oiseaux* (*The Natural History of Birds*) which the comte du Buffon wanted to be exhaustive and which remained interminable.

—

If "the role of the poet is to say not what really happened but what one can expect,"[18] the reversal of the body in time rejects

15. "Le mouvement de l'histoire, l'ambition historienne ne sont pas l'exaltation de ce qui s'est véritablement passé, mais sa néantisation." (*The movement of history, historian ambition, are not the exaltation of what really took place, but its annihilation.*) Pierre Nora, "Entre Mémoire et Histoire," in *Les lieux de la mémoire*. Gallimard. Paris, 1984 (xx).

16. "I CAN STILL SEE YOU : an echo, / palpable with feeler- / words, at the farewell- / ridge. // Your face shies quietly, / when suddenly / light brightens lamplike / inside me, at that place / where most painfully one says Never." Paul Celan in *Lightduress*, tr. Pierre Joris. Green Integer. København & Los Angeles, 2005 (99).

17. Gilles Bentz. "18 mars 1967, Torrey Canyon" in *L'oiseau magazine*, no. 126 (printemps 2017) (36).

18. Aristote. *La poétique* [335-323 ? AEC], tr. J. Hardy [1932]. Gallimard. Paris, 1996 (93).

the narrative which is its own by rights, by pulling it down against a posthumous advance. Even if these "painful efforts are vain,"[19] they condition the casting-off of distances, and the fugitive repatriations. Only then is one within one's rights to evoke traversals : in other words their impediment. By placing their mouths fatally upon "the mouth of misfortunes that have no mouth."[20]

The reading of a text is a posthumous event. And the gaze is the capricious reminder of a perpetual belatedness.[21] To seize the instant in its flight, is to brush up against a fossilized era, and to advance along a road is to disavow the future out of which it is made.[22] The name says nothing other than

---

19. ": un rocher naissant remplacera le rocher qui s'écroule, détruit par des milliers d'années d'un pénible travail, et l'océan, toujours immense, couvrira de ses lames irritables toujours la même immensité." Claude Cahun. *Vues et visions, op. cit.*, p. 100 [78]. (: *an incipient rock will replace the rock that is crumbling, destroyed by thousands of years of painstaking work, and the ocean, always immense, will cover with its irritable blades always the same immensity.*) But also : "Et ce fameux rocher, il est très simple de le pulvériser en mille morceaux. Avec de la poudre. La preuve, les hommes ne cessent de tout détruire, jusqu'à de hautes montagnes." Kawabata Yasunari, *Tanpopo* (*Les pissenlits*), tr. Hélène Morita. Albin Michel. Paris, 2012 (186). (The English translation registers significant enough variances in emphasis and tone to reproduce both versions here: *Even that rock—we could smash it to pieces, just like that. A bit of gunpowder is all it would take. People destroy great mountains all the time, one after the next.* Tr. Michael Emmerich).

20. Aimé Césaire. *Cahier d'un retour au pays natal.* Présence Africaine. Paris / Dakar, 1983 (22).

21. A time overturned, and without antecedent because always on the verge of arrival, with recaptured delay.

22. Claude Cahun: "(Ce garçon) ressemblait aux portraits d'Antinoüs. Il avait, dans la fierté, la violence, l'aisance et la gaucherie de son comportement, dans la sauvagerie qui semblait l'incliner vers la solitude, quelque chose de mystérieux [...]." (*[This boy] resembled the portraits of Antinoüs. There was, in his pride, his violence, the ease and awkwardness of his bearing, in the savagery that seemed to dispose him to solitude, something mysterious [...].*) *Lettre à*

its desuetude, and this is true also, for the "cities, mirrors, agonies"[23] whose reflected image insinuates a clandestinity at work. The congealments that inspire horror smothered by movement, beat with a pulse whose intimacy belongs to the buried course of submerged lands, to a vitality anterior to itself. Little obsolete body to which is owed the last word of *liberty*.

(June 2019)

Gaston Ferdière, mars 1946, in *Écrits*, *op. cit.* (674).
23. Paul Virilio. *L'insécurité du territoire* [1976]. Galilée. Paris, 1993 (15).

REPATRIATION -- fire to the sea

—*But what on earth has happened to you ? Now that I see you, I tell myself that nothing in particular happened, but when the one who must come doesn't arrive, it is, how can I put it, a strangely sad thing.*

KAFŪ

Once and for all amounts to never. It isn't a question, nor a remonstrance, nor even a manner of foreclosing. And if the emotion assumes the form of an architecture, it is evidence that its structure is lacking the error out of which it is made. I was that emissary. If the letter is water, it is dry at present, memory of water and desire for stone, one less effigy, a music, in other words minor in the depth of its secret and silence of abatement. Snow of mud in which to walk running to sinking, an arm, mine, burst from the deep, you drown inhaling a tomb of ice to the end of your thinking. A field of fairies you say, the day darkens under the fires of flies, but undermine yourself, it's a day like another, softly shredded. You cross, then, you run, sideways, you cut short and reduce the duration, without recusing a thing, you say (it isn't a reflection), fast, I go, and what narrows is not the area, its surface, but the gaze in its depth. You go down, several strata, the area is such that it swallows into you. And this arm, telescopic stem, you make yourself flower, or free fall (without wings or beating), is unprecedented because ignored. No hand seizes yours, save one, and the more you inhale, the more you swim, the more you slide, and the idea of an outcome collides with the walls progressively closing the lungs by which you palpitate, run shivers through the calm, you vest yourself vertically. That. You see it coming, under the trap of ice, under the cloud of snow whose porosity extends your state of suspension, there, I mean nowhere, in the fragile envelope of frigatebirds, I mean its lightness. You had dreamt flooding, a water of devouring fire, and the forest crumbling under the cries of threadbare birds. But it is a livid plain of sky and surface, where a single fence bordered by footsteps assembles the reckoned absences; you, go quickly, you turn and return, you want to catch yourself up, so you run, after the other one who moves along into the realms of fugitive sandpipers, you don't wait to think, the sky is dim, grey like your hands which clutch at the air, you step over the hidden ditch, the cavern or the well, you step over the precipitous wait, you are once again late, assimilated in the mezzanine of no thinking, between snow and mud, countermanded. It is an indiscretion to run so, to one's ruin, short of breath, as though the Louvre opened its doors to you alone, you as well as the blue wing of Samothrace, level with the sea, knot by knot, as far as the crumbling staircase.

. . . .
. . . .

Who do you think you are talking to? You see him come, you tell yourself, this is the way by which it doesn't happen. You sense and feel it into the absence of a name to shout out. It is not worth the trouble. Your disappointment is without importance, you resemble the rivulet of water infiltrating the cobbles toward a complex system of secreted channels. It is confirmed, there is no firmament. You say so to no one resolutely. You say it, you encounter yourself nowhere. You are hounded into the obsolete *e* hanging from the window with the threat of letting it fall, nominal bit of detritus, petty capital pains. It was not knowing or being able even to admit what could only be summed by ignorance. The hooves still resound in the narrow pathways of moist cities where you have watched yourself hurry along, awkwardly, and without lightness, in the shadows of cathedrals, oh what im-*pertinence*, and the sea retreated all the way to the mountainsides. You saw them in the cemeteries, north and south, pinned to the walls like bats, full of fear into their livid eyes, hanging by their manes and each of them trembling in the stinging wind of the ministries. Common grave, *not I*. I recuse the partition of the erst. You quicken with the bodies that come out of the earth. Two feet, not four. So what? An afflicted mathematics. Emptied of its armature. Never do you set tooth against bone or hand to fire, you have no care for the blind city. What is to be, if not ruin yourself at the pronominal game? At all, you say, as though to escape from your sentence. *I'll get rid of it*. Apprenticeship is a dry swallow of clearings and uprootings and installations each more suspect than the other. And what strain? Filiation is a mire, and if the mire is courting you, alone, you have unattached yourself from the second-hand liars and serial killers. From M to the little girl, your neighbour across the hall, at the other end of the load-bearing world. We is a fine mouth stuffed full of future and regret. Through the door and upstairs, out of mind, ejected. (   ) You mine and undermine, alike. The word *incarnata* is offered by night in the open, you don't want it, you call up and masticate, you lay out and you transpire, you grasp the error that advocates, still the word persists, *incarnata*, like so many incisures in the facture of your sentiment, high on its plied stem, its silks and its pods, filaments of wind and termination, *incarnata* which you are not and picks you off at the antipodes of the pleasurous cry of the secreted tree, with your two unworldly hands, fascicules of pressed voids, the sole mastery of its word is the admission of a crime and its banality. *Yourself, you say, you, you attempt this speaking, say at the top of your teetering voice, my voice, you say, my voice is not a voice, and if you do not believe me, listen some to what manages to come out of me, this sort of dejection of fluids, of seepings through walls, of drownings at the heights of sounds, and of spat syllables, soaked and morne, detestable and threatened, for good speak, by the voice itself the body retrieved, by hands which are not yours, a body that can no longer swim, and chokes on the effort of not screaming, striking or falling sway, just say, as though it were a thing, say, with a voice, worse even than breathing, say the effort of speaking, without words and without vocabulary, a cavalcade of channels, a series of mechanisms, of waiting and desistance, of burst windows, without avowal and without reclamation, not even a sentence or a place name, a name of a name or direction or acquiescence, the voice is not a voice, what is it to make of the end of its sentence, understood and expired, the enterprise of its perennity, the extinction that says a voice, without a mine and without an explosion.* **FILM** The air is yellow, dry, the wind blows hard, the grasses lie flat even though not visible, lie flat on the hill, the hill that could be the prow of a boat, the water is of earth, and the body is standing, the face effaced by the wind, and the sky, somewhere blurred, the features are thick, waves of wind, in every direction, a body in the wind, but human body, abject, then, and suspect, by its verticality, even sitting, with and without the arms by which it is condemnable, from scalp to shoe, naked or dressed, dead or threatened, it is a silent film, erase everything, start over with the horse, the horse, in other words the space made for it, if ever it passes through, and the camera would do well to close its eyes. **FILM** By night, gently. **FILM** *Did Samothrace know how to swim?*

He was made to swallow back all the words that had spoken him. An impetus that came from his proximity to pain, his defeat. He left his mountain, he spat in the sea, he exhausted his reasonings, he espoused a river. As for the war, he didn't count on it, nor the lit path that led to the killing fields. But he became unsparing with his only renewed season. And his heart beat on the wrong side of his body. He carried one upon his shoulder, for twelve years, between two little beds. He harvested his breath at the surface of a mirror, and watered his garden with it just before leaving. The day on which he boarded the boat, he made a single wish that he soon buried. Soon, which is to say after all, alone at his window, he saw that the world was passing and the street had become ever and more filthy, the walls all around him had the same colour and the water stagnated in the canal with the dead birds. In his bedroom he believed many times in nothing, and desiring this nothing he was sullen. It was a terminal cold but which would prolong itself, from mouth to mouth and from refusal to refusal. *What do you know of what undoes you?* The name came out of its place to enter into another body. As far as you could you carried it.

—— —— ——

September, month of silence that precedes silence, free fall of the calendar and who will take it and carry it to the furthermost limit, capsize, love of absence in anticipation, incontinence of a corpse enclosed in its self far from what it had imagined for itself as arrival or departure. The augustment, already, had anticipated this, its sap coagulated in the thin members of interlaced marsh plants, the sun drenched in its illumined exhaustion, and a footstep sunken into the moist earth without delimitation. To walk without knowing. From border to border to the collapse gathered into a self. Why, otherwise, these arms. Why, otherwise, the torn wings of monarchs thrown against some shore and whose trace subsists furled in the seeping leaf of the asclepias. The drainage of the river, the desistance of the beach, the amaranth relieved of its moorings and rush of roaring skies whose shadows draw their light without ambivalence from the faces.
It was said of the world that it was whole and that what exceeded it was given not to be shown. And the snail lived in its spit, and the desert seeped on some humid days, and the wind blew flush

with the earth. The law of compromission imagined itself to be exclusive without admitting to it, and the bodies amassed, one after another, bodies without breath, obliterated or smothered, and loving them was out of the question.

"We won't go." No indication that the sentence was spoken, never mind felt. The cemeteries, evacuated because of illness, invasion, marauding, or flooding, covered an entire surface, a surface of uninscribed stone, rubbed with anger and indifference. Walk there, precisely, without knowing and without inclination. Cross at its exact middle the widest of avenues where the manatees have lost their ocean. Why, otherwise, these arms. A piano without keys, and the hand, irremediable. Dismemberment of a music without a world. And its morne conscription to an unballasted world. The passages have been exceeded, and as to what remains of the rest, it is yet capable of a faint, if not imperceptible, movement, it founders into its foundment which has no name for itself other than ignorance. That one over there, you kissed, and the taste stayed with you, disgust at times, even after having many times dipped your tongue in the salted waters of the pond.

— — —

The thing that is happening to you, you experience it as a sort of skinning, fish or bird, you soar, water. It is a hunger, that comes out of a book to dig into your stomach, where in a dream you saw a pair of scissors planted, a dream that dreamed you into the folds of your slivered skin. It isn't death, you say (you won't look at me), it's the rounding of forms, the cloud that covers the eye that insists it sees the fog in which it is enveloped, and opening the window, absorbs itself into that fog without nonetheless falling; for a long time he dove, he saw himself thrown, vomitted, he was projected against a ground or a mountainside, he rushed, and now that he is aloft (you look at me again), you don't recognise yourself, say it, *admit that you don't recognise yourself* in the slow and delicate footfall, no fracture, no fist closed on nothing, a hatred, perhaps, why not, a history. This history, you say in the air, no wonder, and whether you are being listened to or heard, this history, the one that turns over, and carries all the histories together, the acacias in the book as tall as a bear cub and which fed the dying giraffes of the savannah, the plains dusted by the harvesters long since depleted, this history is the same body that has left you, and which you have ceased to enter for having asphyxiated at such length, kissing it with your mouth and wrapping it in your outskirts, running it over with your regrets and your bursts of rage. What body if not the unanimously assassinated body. (I go out before you say so.)

I have no identity. What I have is the history that cuts through me with its itineraries. Identical to I who am but a series of postponed departures, of blocked roads, of burst dams, of rising waters, muddy and stinking. Identical, I am, and without identity, this is as I want myself, in the mouth of the one that wants to close me, lay me out, suffer me and drag me deep into a night made of flights and strangulation. Of stairs that go down and hands that retrieve, of anemones that burn with their fragility. You, that you say, as you would give death to the first named. And let him answer to satisfy his reprimand. It is for the one who doesn't answer, to you obliquely, un-nominated and free to circulate from outpost to outpost, identical to the unreflexive name, mirrorless, and far from the sandy wanderments. Out of this silence, nothing exits nor enters, and what grows, and is unleashed, has in appearances only one life and a single idea by which, endlessly, it is pursued. The idea of an idea of having been as far as the nothing that awaited there. If once, I had written you, if myself I had called out to you, in the same night that you were moving through, if I cried out to hear myself appeal to you, to tear something from the enormity, and if I bled at the place of my arrival, tell me that you knew nothing of this thing nor of my traversal, because blood is nothing, and to cry out is to pervert oneself with hope and cruelty, to anchor oneself to this unmoored place where the ships one day or another will disappear in the surf, dissolve into the water, identical to the insolence of the tides.

— — —

you walk
you go out
in the burn
of the sun

— — —

He says: *you are still there*. You do not understand the sense of the sentence. You say: *still how*. Like before, he says, there. In your hand there is the white stone of dusk, the memory of the animal, the fire of the sun resorbed by a gaze that cannot be your own. A gaze, what if, incinerated. You do not say the word: incinerated. He goes to leave without moving. He points at something with a finger. A way to convince you that what he says is true. There isn't *still*, you say, but you would like to scream it until the stems that connect your lungs to your voice are severed. You pick up the violin in the middle of the forest, you draw the bow. You make it such that the silence and the instrument are one, without breaking anything. In the room there are several erstwhiles already, the hand held the bow and beat down. You laughed, full of stupor, you laughed loud, and the bigger the laugh in the music hall, the more the bow beat against your shin, the force of music is that. The cello, the viola, attuned to the form of that beating, the vibration of bone struck by the music of that enclosure. You say: *it's like that*. The fingers broken by the piano. The shin bruised by the bow. The head nowhere. You believe you have a better understanding of the word: *still*. But in a way that cannot at all be translated by the sentiments of the everyday. *A wall*, you say, *is a wall*. And you praise the wall that surrounds the garden inside of which the music of the forest cannot be heard. He says he does not follow, and yet in him is the same forest also but it is not a forest *still*. How do you spell it, you check the dictionary, it isn't made for this kind of consultation. Where was I when I was summoned for the first time?

— — —

someone
comes through
and closes all
the doors

— — —

It is no longer a letter but an observation. It is not either possible to refer to oneself as *inconsolable* or even in the grips of *disconcertion* or *failure*; even capsized a ship is still a ship, even shattered a stone is recognisable by its shards. And annihilation is a big word for the slow dilapidation at the end of which your name arrives, wiped of its blood, disabused of its initial desire, rendered, as are you, in other words put back in your place, stripped of your competence, gently crushed by a slight pressure that breaks you here or here. And the need to stop it. To serve as a construction in order to deduce its superfluity. For the unconsoled is yet seduced by the hope procured in aching, the assurance of dying of a premature death, she will live anew and better, spirited and driven, softened by distress and the one who waits. If you have travelled like the tree, you have floundered like the most miscreant of mariners, rubbed rough, and avid for your ascendency, palpitant and sweating, and cursing your intention: *exhaust me!* the echo of which is a dull thud against the four walls of a room without you. You say a thing that covers you in blisters, and with each piece of skin, and lowly wound, you recognise pain for what it is: an insignificant breathless tirade.

— — —

It is only when you enter the room that you become aware of the lack of interest of the thing. It could happen the other way around, when leaving. It is the movement which doesn't declare itself that is so staggering. You say the word *vertiginous*. You catch yourself. It's nothing. Or this is as you wish it. You sit on the small step. The house collapses around you. Or this is as you wish it. And for the sky to tear in a very immediate way. In this you are right to belie yourself. Because what you say is such a tiring banality. Say you fall in the stairs. The body escapes you, yours or another, and the cry resonates in the elevatorless shaft. It falls and you cry out. And nothing happens. You pick yourself up. You pick yourself up, and you go. Otherwise who will look after the body. All of this is a false testimony, of course, including the gunfire. You understand that the historian, when he is cut down, says nothing. And what he doesn't say is imagined by no one, including yourself. On your way up the stairs, when throwing yourself into the ditch, you repeat nothing, you humiliate your idea of suffering. All that has been dug or buried, inhumed or forbidden returns to you in its nullity. The law is made for that. For the rewriting of your fear, and the dissolution of your defenses. All masks are mortuary, and the faces are of wax, and the cities were once swamps where the poets died a just death, blinded and gagged.

— — —

The first blow arrives from inside. I stagger. The tree that grows from the belly of the bird suffers from its migrations. There were so many abolished correspondences that you don't trust them anymore. North or south, and along those highways where nothing grows. You get down and you can't remember. You ask to be told, but who, there isn't. It isn't a word, you say, *it isn't a word*. So never mind then. Without the word there is nonetheless the thing and the matter isn't settled. A threat hovers, always the same, it avoids your dreams at present, it settles blatantly on the little table. Next it disappears. The path you take is an apocryphal path. You tire of it. You run, finally, out of boredom, you run all the way to me. *Let me tell you: me, is a pretty big word. The dune, you do not climb, not in the dream nor at the end of the highway where the signs indicate* FORBIDDEN, *even if you see yourself deep inside it already, the dune, with your ears and your anus full of sand and your body suspended in that friable matter, light, and dense, and formless, shot through with the vibrations of the nuclear power plant. The water quivers just like your pelvis, broken, counterfeit. You choke not for having swallowed this sand, which will soon be mud, but for having stayed on so long. In your dreams, the real ones, you break the windows, but they glue themselves back together before you are able to throw yourself through them.*

—— —— ——

The reversal of perspective requires of the uprooted tree that it grow inward and of the eye that it be discharged of its objectivity. A funeral march takes the path of a coast scattered with unruptured shells, arm in arm as far as the expected precipice. The call vests itself in such ransoms, excavating the interstices, and its span is reduced without conceding anything of its power, in flight as under cover. It was said of those heads that they had made an about-turn, that the contingent of congealed bodies given to confronting the tidal wave, had turned around twice and that before the eyes of all, scorned, their inertia had intensified, bringing to a liquid surface the buried mineral deposit serving as their foundment. And that imperceptibly, without a shudder nor a quiver, they had set about walking, re-versing themselves progressively into the surf, and taking with them unto the very last fluttering leaf of the island.

—— —— ——

A rupture grabs hold of the continuities. A roof deployed reveals what remains of the removed body. Whatever the case, a kidnapping always takes place during the day, in the middle of the crowd, where the perambulations are either slow or rushed but always indifferent as to the context. Bodies, buildings, atmospheric changes. The cry, isolated from its place, is given to a void and never travels far, it is extinguished. In any case, it is foregone. And you who speed along untiringly, you know better than anyone, in other words: *not in the least*. The era of protestation has ended in absolute obedience. The white flag, waved in desperation, is also a shroud, it lacks only a corpse, but it will turn up, of course, stained with the blood of its fellow citizens.

— — —

Out of the name that by its own admission is intolerable, it becomes evident that even an annihilated body prefers its suppression to the reduction of its movements. So it relegates itself to a mistaken itinerary, it chooses destitution, it says *I* to the point of depletion without evoking an anterior state, a fixed address, the dislocation of its articulations undermined by one or several forms of hesitation, a hastened acceptation of a disavowed watchword. Whereas the ceiling was falling in, the film was shot in the dark, the window, pierced by a bullet, allowed for the infiltration of what was assuredly atomic light, and the cracked stones registered the footsteps, not those of an undeclared birth year, but those of a desperate architecture, and body drowned at the edge of an inventoried beach assigned to another continent. It had been necessary to travel far, all the way to the finished city in order to accuse the great delay that reigned there, unto the garden of toppled statues, where one's sole means of survival is to steal from oneself.

— — —

Why tell such things? This is the way of memory: in the twenty years between myself and a city, only the city remained, with its names and its injuries. It is not me, walking, nor even a phantom, but a form of eradication that bears the cost of this much walking out. When the Austrian philosopher declares that "a man will be *imprisoned* in a room with a door that's unlocked and opens inwards; as long as it does not occur to him to *pull* rather than to push it," he overlooks the problem of indifference, which is this: that a bullet fired at glass will transpierce the body in the way of its shattering.

— — —

To you, I declare myself missing. I remove my name from the registers. I empty the shelves of the burned books. I cut the hands of the petrified lovers. I return the caress to the bottoms of the oceans. I slide into the interstice of the cargo. I see the human furled there. And the snails. And the anger that is erased from the most bruised surfaces of the inhumed territories. I walk, and I swim. I sink the raft with the sun. I burn the bones of my face. I crumble the coasts of the continents. I run far in the wind. I fall back.

— — —

When did you first adopt the past as a mode of the conditional? And to speak yourself, like the burnt filament, a light long since extinguished, but whose shadow persists as though to inter its debilitated memory. It is a manner of live burial, something that beats the blood of the livid organism. You are that shadow, but there is no one left to say so, your language was unique, and so resisted its extension into other avid mouths, filed against a time in which your refusal was your sole designation, but not only. Of the syncope you made an outcome leading to a place of stumbling, in which step by step, you could advance yourself, without nonetheless managing to wrest yourself completely from your incandescence; an incandescence that is at once dull and unconscious, and whose true sun pitilessly carbonises the skin in which you are wrapped like the film in the casing behind its lens. You are water, water that burns, into the coursing channels and the ardour of the seas exhausted by the wave that strikes and propulses, into the fracturing of the continents. *It is the same sky, but it is not the same discernment. I even heard you say: My known name is bound to the gallows. It is fatal.*

— — —

that which
in me
abides

— — —

Still you have no sense of the white inks' intensity. What of the word malheur in relation to these? Blindness, insomnia. You leave, knowing that you belong to his death already.

— — —

My wounded heart fears seeing the willow before the door.
—Mao K'ouen

— — —

this   word
mal   heur

— — —

The body in flesh just as it touches the mortiferous water emerges of stone, statufied by its disappearance, and to which it owes its singularity. I was of that tribunal, Antinoüs. Like you, I gave of my name.

— — — — — — — — — — — — — — —

The moon each night releases me into the dream.

— — — — — — — — — — — — — — —

He saw what others had seen before him. So the present escaped him into its luminosity, attenuated such as it was. Being born had no meaning, since the itinerary he had chosen for himself, or that he had taken on, denied him all recourse to reflexivity, *me I.* He was aware, if needed be, of the futility of his advancement in time, since time had already caught up with him, and there was a consensus around him as to his obsolescence. He regretted nonetheless that he would not be able to read at leisure the mail that would be addressed to him after his death. His suicide letter would be the ultimate conviction that in the end his life will have been made of letters sent without a hope for a reply and of musics played on shattered keyboards, with broken chords such as those used to tie up prisoners or to hang the accused. When, in a moment of distraction, he lowered his head over a river, while standing on one of those bridges that were fast being demolished, instead of seeing the water, he saw the bodies buried there, and this amounted to a lot of bodies at the end of a life that had no hope of catching up with itself.

Il faut accepter la dernière bouchée   puis reposer la main
et cesser de traduire.

Frédérique Guétat-Liviani

Credits

DISPATCH FOR AN EARLY GRAVE—written at a time of great noise, the author chose not to publish this work before today. Even so, the silence it carries stands in defence of solitude. It becomes eventually apparent that the mob stands on both sides of the barricade.

AUGUSTMENT (TRANSLATION WITHOUT LANGUAGE) was first published in a limited-edition chaplet by Belladonna (2015). A version was subsequently included in Jane Joritz-Nakagawa's anthology *women: poetry: migration* (theenk books, 2018).

HATRED OF TRANSLATION was commissioned by Jeffrey Zuckerman for publication in *Music & Literature* (2015).

Solicited by Adam Morris and Bruno Carvalho, DERELICT OF DUTY was written for *Essays on Hilda Hilst: Between Brazil and World Literature* (London: Palgrave Macmillan, 2017).

First presented as part of a Translating Transgender workshop held in 2015 at the University of Arizona in Tucson, "PLUS THE SWINGING OF THE DOOR" was published with some adjustment in *Transgender Studies Quarterly* (Duke University Press, 2016; vol. 3/3-4).

SMALLPOX FOR THE MILLENARY was first published as an afterword to Alain Jugnon's *a body, in spite* (Nightboat Books, 2017).

THE SOLITARY DEATHS OF MIZOGUCHI KENJI re-writes in English a discarded dictionary entry intended for the *Dictionnaire Deleuze* (Robert Laffont, 2020). Its first publication was in *Seedings* at the invitation of Jerrold Shimona.

The texts collected under the title [A]VERSIONS—A DELIBERATIVE DOSSIER, were respectively spoken or published as follows:

"WE GIVE OUR LIVES FOR NOTHING" was the text for a film seminar held in June 2017 at the School of the Art Institute of Chicago accompanying a screening of Kobayashi Masaki's *Kabe atsuki heya* (in English as *The Thick-Walled Room*, 1956 [1953]).

ALULA, FOR POSTERITY (AUTOBIOGRAPHY OF TRANSLATION) was published in a much-reduced form by *North American Review* (2018) in connection with a translation dossier edited by Joyelle McSweeney. The long version reproduced here, with some adjustment, was the text of a talk given at Glendon College (Toronto) in November 2017, at the invitation of Elena Basile.

THE OPEN, UNDER COVER was the text of a talk given in December 2017 at the Spertus Institute (Chicago) in the context of a dialogue with Matthew Girson organised by Ruslana Richtzier.

ADDENDUM—OF THE TWO GARDENS, rewrites in English the French introductory passage to "Alula, de son nom de plume", a text spoken in November 2017 at the Centre Anne-Hébert at Université de Sherbrooke under Nicole Côté's hospitality.

ARRÊT SUR VISAGE accompanies Nathanaël's translation of *In the Environs of a Film*, a triad of posthumously published texts by Danielle Collobert (Litmus Press, 2019). A version of these notes was published, at Kyoo Lee's invitation, in *PhiloSOPHIA* (Spring, 2019).

EFFACEMENTS—TURNS, TO TORN SUNS was the text for a film seminar accompanying a 16-mm screening of *Kuratta ichipeiji* (*A Page of Madness*) by Kinugasa Teinosuke (text by Kawabata Yasunari) at the School of the Art Institute of Chicago in June 2018.

An abbreviated version of THE TIME OF EXPOSURE IS NEVER was the talk for a film seminar following a 16mm screening of *Le sang d'un poète* by Jean Cocteau at the School of the Art Institute of Chicago in June 2019.

A reduced version of REPATRIATION—FIRE TO THE SEA was first published in the exhibition catalogue *Enrico David: Gradations of Slow Release* (2018), at the invitation of Michael Darling (Museum of Contemporary Art, Chicago).

For their generosity and confidence, the author is grateful to the editors, scholars and curators who initiated the aforementioned convergences.

Translations

The epigraph by René Char on the verge of this work translates as "One cannot go mad in a fanatical age even though one can be burned alive by a fire that is equal to oneself."

The epigraph by Kawabata (165) is translated by J. Martin Holman.

The epigraph by Kafū (181) is rendered in English after Alain Nahoum's French translation.

The closing epigraph by Frédérique Guétat-Liviani (199) translates as "One must accept the last mouthful   then set the hand down / and stop translating."

Unattributed translations throughout are by Nathanaël.

Images

Cover: "Courly [sic] rouge du Brésil, âgé de trois ans" by François-Nicolas Martinet (1725?-1800), Imprimerie Royale, 1783, 32 cm X 22 cm, print (colour aquarelle engraving). Conservation: Conseil général de La Réunion, Muséum d'Histoire naturelle de La Réunion (Inventory n° 314-Pl.81). Reproduced with permission.

pp. 31 + 40: From the *(rejet apparent)* series by Nathanaël (2013-2014). Black and white (analog) photograph.

p. 70: Vévé (religious symbol) of the Marassa. Artist unknown.

pp. 99 + 105: "Sugamo Prison on December 22, 1948", Photographer unknown. Published in *Asahi Historical Photographs Library: War and People 1940-1949*, Volume 5. Publisher: Asahi Shimbun Company. Photograph is in the public domain.

p. 147: From the *Murmurations* series by Nathanaël (2016). Black and white (analog) photograph.

This work does not predispose itself to dedication,
and yet I wish to name, for their friendship,
and acuity, Daniel Eisenberg,
Reginald Gibbons, Jennifer Scappettone.

Other works by Nathanaël

D'un geste décidé. Fidel Anthelme X. Marseille, 2018.

La mort de ma sœur. Dernier Télégramme. Limoges, 2018.

Pasolini's Our. Nightboat Books. New York, 2018.

Alula, de son nom de plume. L'Hexagone. Montréal, 2018.

Le cri du chrysanthème. Le Quartanier. Montréal, 2018.

N'EXISTE Carnets 2007-2010. Le Quartanier. Montréal, 2017.

Laisse (rejet apparent). Mémoire d'encrier. Montréal, 2016.

Feder, a scenario. Nightboat Books. New York, 2016.

L'heure limicole. Fidel Anthelme X. Marseille, 2016. Prix Claudine de Tencin.

The Middle Notebookes. Nightboat Books. New York, 2015. Publishing Triangle Award.

Asclepias, the Milkweeds. Nightboat Books. New York, 2015.

Sotto l'immagine. Mémoire d'encrier. Montréal, 2014.

Sisyphus, Outdone. Theatres of the Catastrophal. Nightboat Books. New York, 2012.

Carnet de somme. Le Quartanier. Montréal, 2012.

Carnet de délibérations. Le Quartanier. Montréal, 2011.

We Press Ourselves Plainly. Nightboat Books. New York, 2010.

Carnet de désaccords. Le Quartanier. Montréal, 2009.

Absence Where As (Claude Cahun and the Unopened Book). Nightboat Books. Callicoon, (NY), 2009.

At Alberta. BookThug. Toronto, 2008.

...s'arrête? Je. L'Hexagone. Montréal, 2008. Prix Alain-Grandbois.

The Sorrow And The Fast Of It. Nightboat Books. New York, 2007.

L'Absence au lieu (Claude Cahun et le livre inouvert). Nota bene. Montréal, 2007.

Touch to Affliction. Coach House Books. Toronto, 2007.

Je Nathanaël. BookThug. Toronto, 2006; Book*hug & Nightboat Books. Toronto & New York, 2018.

L'INJURE. L'Hexagone. Montréal, 2004.

Paper City. Coach House Books. Toronto, 2003.

Je Nathanaël. L'Hexagone. Montréal, 2003.

L'embrasure. Éditions TROIS. Laval (Qc), 2002.

Somewhere Running. Arsenal Pulp Press. Vancouver, 2000.

UNDERGROUND. Éditions TROIS. Laval (Qc), 1999; Le Quartanier. Montréal, 2018.

Colette m'entends-tu? Éditions TROIS. Laval (Qc), 1997.

NIGHTBOAT BOOKS, a nonprofit organization, seeks to develop audiences for writers whose work resists convention and transcends boundaries. We publish books rich with poignancy, intelligence, and risk. Please visit nightboat.org to learn about our titles and how you can support our future publications.

The following individuals have supported the publication of this book. We thank them for their generosity and commitment to the mission of Nightboat Books:

Kazim Ali
Anonymous
Jean C. Ballantyne
Photios Giovanis
Amanda Greenberger
Elizabeth Motika
Benjamin Taylor
Peter Waldor
Jerrie Whitfield & Richard Motika